No Stranger

Tat Stewart

Copyright © 2023 Tat Stewart

All rights reserved.

ISBN: 978-1-7342871-4-1

DEDICATION

To my life partner and best friend, Patty Stewart, for all the support and inspiration she has been to me throughout our marriage.
I couldn't have lived this life without you.

TABLE OF CONTENTS

Foreword by Patty Stewart — Pg 2

Words of Praise for <u>No Stranger</u> — Pg 8

Chapter One: You Have to Leave — Pg 12

Chapter Two: Early Influences — Pg 22

Chapter Three: Mashhad — Pg 32

Chapter Four: Life in Tehran — Pg 40

Chapter Five: My Identity — Pg 48

Chapter Six: Seminary — Pg 56

Chapter Seven: Going to Iran — Pg 64

Chapter Eight: Ministering to a Church in Crisis — Pg 72

Chapter Nine: The Next Generation — Pg 84

Chapter Ten: Go Home! — Pg 96

Chapter Eleven: What Now? — Pg 104

Chapter Twelve: The Birth of an Iranian Church — Pg 110

Chapter Thirteen: The Diaspora — Pg 124

Chapter Fourteen: The Explosive Growth of Christianity — Pg 138

Chapter Fifteen: The Challenges of the Great Awakening — Pg 146

Chapter Sixteen: Pressing On For His Glory — Pg 154

Appendix: The Keys to the Iranian Heart — Pg 162

Ministry Resources by Tat Stewart — Pg 174

ACKNOWLEDGMENTS

Mr. Sourik Saiadian, President of the Jude Project, for his invaluable encouragement and partnership in the tedious process of publishing my book.

Rev. Mansour Khajehpour for his valuable assistance in fact checking and helpful suggestions.

A very special thanks to Emily Stewart, my daughter, for all the hours she put in as my editor and to Patty Stewart, my wife, for all time she spent on putting the finishing touches on my book.

FOREWORD
by Patty Stewart

After meeting Tat Stewart for the first time, I was left speechless. Was it a sudden wave of shyness? Was it his overwhelming charm? Or was it because I was only two weeks old and hadn't yet learned to speak any words—crying was my only means of communication up to this moment. I don't remember if I cried at our meeting. In fact, I don't remember anything! He, being older and wiser by two years, likewise has no recollection of that moment. Probably that is for the best — I was completely bald.

Our mothers, Nancy Murray and Natalie Stewart, had recently met each other in Tehran in 1948 at a special conference for first-term missionaries to Iran. They had quickly bonded and my mother asked the question: "Would you like to see my new baby?" That question can never politely be answered by anything but "Yes, of course!" Tat came along because his mother was carrying him so he had no say in the matter. Not the stuff of romantic boy-meets-girl stories, exactly.

The next time I saw him was in my home city of Mashhad. He was now a tall twelve-year-old with dark, soulful brown eyes staring at me; I was ten years old and not impressed — he stood as stiff as a statue. Later he confessed he had been terrified; I was a girl, a species he had been unfamiliar with for the most part. I flounced off to ride bikes with the Iranian boys in the missionary compound we all lived in. He was obviously not my type.

We would meet up again when both of us were sent to Tehran to attend Community School and live in the newly-built boarding house for missionary children. It was located on the sprawling compound of a former Christian hospital which now served as a school with over two hundred students representing thirty nationalities. There were thirteen of us missionary ("mish") kids living in the boarding house which was overseen by Park and Alice Johnson, two brave souls who were willing to take on the daunting task of supervising, feeding and disciplining such a diverse bunch, ranging from fifth grade to twelfth.

The girls had rooms on the second floor while the boys were assigned the first floor, making it more convenient for them to sneak out their windows at night during "study hall" to make runs to the corner store (slight resemblance to an American 7-11) purchasing snacks, and returning to the dorm, usually unnoticed. We girls, not to be undone, developed a system using a large metal bucket tied to a rope, which we filled with our written food requests and lowered to the first-floor window. After the boys returned, we would feel a strong tug on the rope, our signal to raise the bucket up to the second story window which would now be filled with chips, cokes and candy. What thoughtful boys, you might say! But they knew their nightly snack runs would be over if we ever told "Aunt Alice," so their generosity was a small price to pay for our silence.

Tat began sitting next to me during meal times—two large tables covered with white cloths took up most of the large dining room. I was thrilled by his warm attention. But I soon learned why: I was a slow eater. He hungrily (he was always hungry, poor guy) eyed my food — "Are you going to eat those potatoes?" "Do you want your dessert?" Since by now I had a big crush on him, believing "the way to a man's heart is through his stomach", I gladly sacrificed my "extras." He told me years later that that was what first attracted him to me. And I had thought it was my fun personality and budding beauty. Sigh.

In 1964, when I was sixteen, my family of six (I had three younger siblings) returned to the United States for good. My dad planned to study psychiatry; his years of surgery and general medical practice in Mashhad and Rasht had challenged him to further his experience. We went home to Denver, Colorado. Tat, eighteen, left Iran the same year with his family, to live in Lambertville, New Jersey. Over 1500 miles now separated us and we lost touch with each other.

In the summer of 1965, however, a beloved mutual friend and former missionary to Iran, Dr. Glen Knecht, happened to be visiting Denver and asked my mother and me to meet him at the airport. My then boyfriend accompanied us. I remembered that Glen was Tat's pastor back in Oxford, Pennsylvania, and innocently asked, "How's Tat?" I quickly forgot his answer, I am embarrassed to admit. I had moved on.

Unbeknownst to me, when Dr. Knecht returned to Pennsylvania he reported to Tat that "Patty is still carrying the torch for you!" Something was rekindled in Tat — I must still like him! Not long afterwards, a letter arrived from Tat containing a nice synopsis of the two years since we had last seen each other. He closed by saying how difficult this Christmas was going to be for him due to the fact that his parents had returned to Iran, so he would have to spend Christmas in an empty dorm. My Mom's instant response after I read it to her was an enthusiastic "Oh, let's invite the big galoot out here!" "What?" I was shocked! I didn't even know him anymore. Mom would hear no objections, so Christmas Eve found my Dad, my sister Sharon, and me greeting him at Stapleton Airport in Denver. Very awkward! We shook hands. I thought, what are we going to do for two weeks living in the same house? He acted twenty years older than me; plus, he seemed terrified of me. The ice melted gradually and we became good friends. He loved our snowy Colorado, our family, and he also began to love me. It was mutual. We spent a wonderful Christmas together. Then reality struck as the two weeks came to a close. How would we be able to be apart now that we had fallen in love? We clung to each other, not knowing where our relationship would go.

After his return to Pennsylvania the letters began to flow between us. Phone calls were far too expensive, so we reserved those for special times. He wrote at least once a day, sometime twice, making even a boring day in classes sound like a love letter. Which they became increasingly. He checked his mailbox daily for signs of my replies, which were not as frequently as his — nursing classes and studying overwhelmed me.

Then in my freshman year of college, *the* letter arrived which shook me to my core. "Dearest Patty, I believe the Lord has called me into the ministry." Oh no, I thought! I can't be a minister's wife! Choose Door #2 please! I love you but I can't do it! I'm too shy and not at all the pastor's wife type! Please NO! I thought you wanted to be an ambassador and travel? How about that? And secondly, I am not spiritual enough! My concept of a minister's wife may have been a bit extreme because my minister's wife in Denver was *perfect*. She baked freezers full of delicious croissant rolls along with delicious meals every Sunday to be delivered to different families, including ours. She was warm and kind to everyone who wanted to talk to her! She dressed impeccably, never even a run in her stockings! She led Bible studies and played the piano! That could never be me! These jumbled thoughts never found their way into a return letter to Tat. Maybe it would be best to end our relationship and slowly go our separate ways. He had chosen his path and it terrified me.

However, without my realizing it, God had long ago chosen me to be a minister's wife. He would mold me into His role for me, and I didn't even have to play the piano!

We chose August 3, 1969 as our wedding day; he would begin seminary in Princeton, New Jersey, while I finished my senior year in Colorado. Yes, we would be apart for most of that year but we knew it was right for us. Then came seminary, our first church, our first baby, Timmy, followed by our daughter, Emily. During this time, our dear friend Dr. William Miller continued to beg us to consider returning to Iran; he reminded us of the desperate need for the Persian people to hear the Gospel. I turned a deaf ear. Had I not already left behind my family in Colorado to live in New Jersey where our new church was? Wasn't that far enough, Lord? And now Iran? With two toddlers? For years??? This time I'll try door #3, please...

Tat was directing a Jr. High camp that summer while I stayed home with little Timmy, age 3 and Emily, 18 months. Another letter arrived. More chills. "Dear Tat, we invite you to become the pastor of Saint Christopher's church in Abadan, Iran..." I had been to Abadan as a teen and remembered well the oil fields with the acrid smells along with the excessively high temperatures and desert-like surroundings. I shuddered at the thought.

However, at that very moment, the Holy Spirit changed my heart completely! "Yes, Lord, I'll go!" Excitedly, I phoned Tat and asked, "How would you like to go to Abadan and be the pastor of St. Christopher's Church?" Dead silence, then... "Patty? Is that you?" "Yes, honey, and I'm ready to go!" I knew it was God's will! Tat never sounded happier! I had kept him too long from what God had called him to do but we were now in agreement and it was thrilling!

You will have to read the rest of this book to know what happened next as well as the rest of our lifelong venture together!

First, though, I would like you to know this man I have known for nearly 75 years. You may already have had that privilege. As his wife, I hope I can show you just a part of what has been the theme of his life, lovingly shared with me. I have chosen five main characteristics to share with you:

- **His passion.** For our Lord, for working for His kingdom, for his family, and his friends.
- **His tireless dedication.** He enthusiastically turns out new sermons continually, as well as Bible studies, online teaching programs, booklets about crucially-needed topics such as the power of forgiveness, the Christian family, finances, and many others.
- **His seriousness.** It had been a challenge for him to join our active, fun-loving family, who loved to laugh and tell jokes! His calm seriousness was a good complement, and often helped me during times of turmoil, as his was usually the voice of logic and reason. Don't get me wrong; he has learned the lighter side of relationships and has a great sense of humor, but it is grounded. I need that.
- **His deep wisdom.** Because of his not being tossed about by surrounding emotions and situations, he sees more clearly what needs to be done or said at the moment, whether in a heated church meeting, a counseling session, or in the case of a broken dishwasher, I have come to rely on his perspective.
- **His servant heart.** His greatest joy is in helping people and being involved in their lives. Whether it is coming early to church to set up chairs and tables, going out of his way to drive people to distant destinations,

shopping for food, or cooking a delicious meal just for me during times of illness or fatigue, he follows Jesus' example of washing His disciples' feet.

Dearest Tat, you have allowed me such a privilege of sharing yourself and your life with me these many years. Throughout times of praying together, laughing, crying, pain, grief, and yet still learning that God has always been in control of everything, I love you more than ever. I love your book, and I am so proud of you and your story.

-Patty Stewart

WORDS OF PRAISE FOR NO STRANGER

No Stranger is a beautiful tale of love and passion for Jesus and for Iran. Tat is an excellent storyteller. As he masterfully shares so many precious memories from the past, you receive deep spiritual nourishment through his great ability to weave different threads from how God sovereignly works through the course of events in his life and ministry. As an Iranian Christian, I enjoyed reading every chapter, every page, and every line that Tat has written. Absolutely brilliant! I recommend No Stranger to all the lovers of Jesus, and to all the lovers of Iran.
With great love and respect.

Rev. Dr. Mehrdad Fatehi
Executive Director, Pars Theological Centre

No Stranger is not solely the story of Rev. Tat Stewart per sé; it is the continuum of God's work in the lives of all missionaries to Iran. It is the fulfilment of the labor of all men and women who left their leisure to serve God among Persians for the last two centuries. No Stranger picks up My Persian Pilgrimage by Rev. Dr. William McElwee Miller and takes it to a new era of evangelicalism in modern age Iran. Filled with humor and humility, this book delineates the example of faithfulness and fidelity for the family of God. I commend this book heartily to all those who are called to serve among the people in the Middle East, especially those who serve among Iranians.

Sourik Saiadian
President, The Jude Project

If I encounter Iranian believers when I travel, the first question I typically ask is whether they have heard of Tat Stewart. The usual response I get is one of mild offense as they politely explain that obviously they know Tat Stewart, as does any respectable Iranian Christian. In my opinion, Tat Stewart is the Billy Graham of the Iranian church, and his recent book, <u>No Stranger</u> portrays an intimate knowledge of not only the Iranian culture but the Spirit's extraordinary work in the Iranian Church. Rev. Stewart both demystifies the reason the Iranian Church is one of the fastest growing churches on earth while equipping the reader to consider how to be a part of this miraculous explosion of the Spirit among the people of Iran.

Alex Pettett
Executive Director of World Witness, Mission board of the Associate Reformed Presbyterian Church

Congratulations on choosing to read this valuable book! You are going to find some very amazing things in these pages. For example, you will see how God works in a person seeking to do the will of God with all his heart even if he is a young and inexperienced novice.

The way is not always clear at first, but Tat (our hero) stays humble and careful until he sees the path God has outlined for him. Tat reveals not only the key stages of his development, but also tells us what spiritual principles he has learned in the process. And he does so in language we can understand.

I have known and loved Tat Stewart since he was a little boy in my Sunday school class in Tabriz, Iran. I have had the joy watching him grow in stature and in favor with God and man. Sometimes we have worked closely together. Often, he sought my counsel and my prayers. And often his guidance to me has proven very helpful. I am honored at his request that I should write these introductory words.

For example, In these wonderful pages we will learn how one can overcome various obstacles in the arduous task of language learning as he gains proficiency in Azari and Farsi at the same time.

Here we will discover the stages of Tat's development as a student of missiology and of Iran. We see effective ministry methods as well as how to avoid common mistakes and pitfalls.

Tat's book motivated me to learn the Persian language more thoroughly. It is an Indo-European tongue which makes it more like our English language. It is not semitic, it is not tonal. It has wonderfully expressive verbs and no lack of strong nouns, giving it the potential of eloquence especially when it contains phrases borrowed from Arabic or French.

So, give this book your close attention. Meditate over its various suggestions and consider what is happening in Tat's mind and heart as he hears and answers the call to serve in Iran.

Consider the large place that the name and person of the Lord Jesus Christ has in

Tat's call and growth in grace. Pray that the Holy Spirit will work in your heart toward your place in the great missionary task of Christ's church.

Dr. Glen Knecht

I enjoyed reading No Stranger, and I think you will find it engaging and informative if you are interested in Iran, the Middle East, or missions.

After a few intense days of post-Islamic revolution till the Stewarts leave Iran for the safety of the United States, the book takes you through the unbelievably harsh journey of a missionary family responding to their call to serve in Iran in the late 40s. Tat's childhood memories and experience growing up in Iran in the early 50s and socializing with locals and other missionaries is captivating and a great insight into the history of Christian Missions in Iran, including Dr. Miller and Dr. Murray's family.

Once you are taken deep into the mission field, the storyline takes a step back into the three generations of Stewarts living in Maryland, how the calling came about, and how they ended up in Iran and not Afghanistan. The details of growing up in a family of six children in an American missionary family, submerged in the Azari culture of Northwest Iran, provide an awesome glimpse into the power of responding to one's calling and passion. A calling that takes an American family from Maryland to Tabriz, to Mashhad, to Tehran, to Hamadan.

The storyline, in addition to the life of service in a distant land, gives the reader an awesome insight into the Eastern culture of honor and shame, as well as Islam's view of Christianity and the obstacles faced witnessing to Muslims of then and now – all in the scope of a Christian Church life in the heartland of Islamic Iran, including the details of daily chores and the horse and buggy ride down the Tabriz main streets. The early experience includes the unfolding of the Iran oil nationalization and a short-lived national revolution followed by the restoration of the Pahlavi dynasty. So many different angles to the storyline that keeps the reader hooked. Experience of Years in Mashhad was especially interesting to me, and I could just close my eyes and see myself there raising and flying the pigeons. The camping by the Akhlamad waterfall brings back memories and a trip down memory lane and the Church of Mashhad, a great introduction to a Church I never knew existed in my hometown.

The details of Tat's spiritual journey leading to Lincoln University, meeting up with his future bride Patty in Denver, working summer at Estes Park, and then being called to ministry and the Princeton seminary. The irony of how Tat's father and his father-in-law were dedicated to serving as missionaries in childhood and how the lives of various men who ended up serving in Iran had crossed over the years back in the US is amazing and a road map of how God prepares and ordains those He calls. The nature of Tat's call to serve Iran and Iranians has taken many different shapes and forms, which gives him great insight into the past, present, and future of the Modern Iranian Church.

This book summarizes Christian missions to Iran from the 40s to the early 80s and the ministry to the Iranians in the US afterward. It seems the location of service for Tat and Patty changed, but the calling and the passion for serving have remained to this day. In addition, it shows a good insight into the Churches in Tabriz, Mashhad, Hamadan, and Tehran, how the Iranian Christian Church took root, and the challenges it faced in the early days of the revolution.

Rev. Dr. Amir Hekmatpour

CHAPTER ONE
YOU HAVE TO LEAVE

"Your eyes saw my unformed substance, in your book were written every one of them, the days that were formed for me when as yet there was none of them."
(Psalm 139:16)

The Tehran streets wound quietly through neighborhoods filled with sleeping residents; but for Patty and me, they were alive with the vivid memories of the recent past months of life in post-Revolutionary Iran. The sounds of honking cars, angry mobs, and the loud chanting of "Death to America!" echoed in our minds as we drove in silence.

As the images of burned-out buildings and graffiti-inscribed walls passed in front of my weary eyes, it occurred to me how they had become the historians recording the events of the Islamic Revolution. The slogans were painted in bright colors, triumphantly declaring such phrases as "Islam is the new order of the day" and "Iran is reveling in bringing the Great Satan to its knees as 52 Americans continued to be held hostage, and President Jimmy Carter seemed helpless to rescue them." I knew that the past months that I had lived in Iran with Patty and my two children would surely not only be unforgettable but also life-changing.

The streets of Tehran had become a stage upon which the politics of a nation had been played out, and we were no strangers to the revolving cast of characters, the scene changes, and the rising emotions of the world audience. Life in Tehran over the past year had made us quite adept at sensing the mood of the city around us. More than once, we had witnessed a seemingly normal street become transformed by a mob of angry Iranians shouting anti-American slogans. Those were times I learned to turn quickly to God in prayer and find alternate routes to my destination.

But now the streets seemed tired and powerless to threaten my peace of mind. The fear that had so often gripped my heart seemed to ebb out of my mind as we drove towards Mehrabad International Airport. The peace I had felt in knowing that we were now on our way out of Iran slowly gave way to new fears about what kinds of challenges we could face at the airport. Persian newspaper articles told of other Americans being exposed as being spies, and I wondered if we might be considered guilty by association and potentially detained on some trumped-up charges. At best, we may be required to endure some delays, which would leave us open to more risk of danger. I breathed a silent prayer, pleading with God that He would enable us all to get out of Iran safely.

The year was 1947 and my life was about to be changed forever. It was a cold and blustery day in December when my parents embarked on their missionary journey to Iran. I was only eighteen months old.

My parents had departed from Philadelphia for the docks of New York city, from which they boarded a WWII troop carrier, "The Marine Carp," and sailed to Beirut, Lebanon and acquired their visas for Iran. Since The Marine Carp had been designed for troops originally, my mother and I were assigned to a room with four large bunk beds, which we shared with Mrs. Dottie Frame[1] and their two children. My mother did not feel well since she was pregnant with my brother Lennie. To make matters more difficult for her, I was sick with a high fever and everyone seemed to be battling seasickness. Dr. John Frame, himself a medical missionary on his way back to Iran with his family and being one of the few who did not get seasick, took over and treated me. He brought down my temperature and may have, in fact, saved my life. I was later, as an adult, able to meet him and thank him for his special care for me on my first trip to Iran.

Upon arriving in Beirut, they took a bus to Baghdad, Iraq. They then rented a car and driver, who delivered them safely over the rugged mountains to Hamadan. We spent some time there at the Hamadan Christian Hospital where Presbyterian missionaries were stationed to train a new generation of Iranians to join their staff. Our fellow laborers warmly welcomed us, and we rested there a few days.

---

1. Dr. Frame's daughter, Margaret Frame, wrote and published a book about their life in Iran, entitled Passage to Persia (available on Amazon).

After a long and tiring drive, we arrived at the outskirts of Tabriz and were greeted there by gently falling snow that was blanketing the dreary mud walls of this ancient city, a city that had once hosted Marco Polo and other great explorers seeking routes to China. But the only thought that occupied my parents' minds was wondering what kind of life lay ahead of them. As it was late afternoon, darkness began to settle over this strange place that would become their new home. As they meandered through the city streets, they realized they did not know how to get to their destination, the Tabriz Christian Hospital. The driver had to find someone near the big covered bazaar who spoke Arabic and he was told where to find the hospital: Shahnaz Avenue. Before long, they pulled up to the big wooden gates of the hospital and were welcomed by the gateman who informed the missionary community that the Stewarts had arrived.

Stewart Family 1947

My parents spent the first six months living with another missionary family, Rev. and Mrs. Liv Bentley, who had been long-time residents of Tabriz. During this period, my parents studied Azeri Turkish[2], the native language of the people of Tabriz. They also realized the many challenges of maintaining a household in a new country. Water had to be boiled before it was safe to drink, and the cook had to shop every day for fresh meat and produce. When the cook returned each day from the bazaar, all of us eagerly greeted him since he brought with him the famous "barbari" bread that would become a staple in the Stewart home. (Barbari is oval shaped flat bread, sprinkled with sesame seeds and baked in a wall oven until the outside is crispy and the inside is soft.)

Having heard my mother's recounting those early days, they were quick learners and soon adjusted to the challenges of a new life. Later, they would move into a small apartment next to the hospital that they rented from the Mayvaians who soon became like family. My earliest memories are from

---

2. People from the Azeri background mainly live in Northwestern Iran and refer to their language as "Turkish" or "Turki" which should not be confused with the language of Turkey. Azeri is also spoken in the country of Azerbaijan.

our time of living in the Mayvaian apartment. Even at the ripe old age of four, I could make my way to the Mayvaian home, timing my visit to coincide with their noon meal. I am sure my love for Iranian food began at that early age. As a child growing up in Tabriz, I was exposed to many languages. Of course, I heard English at home, Turkish from most of the hospital employees and Assyrian from our landlords, and I also had many Armenian friends as well. I became somewhat fluent in most of the languages.

Years later, as I reflected upon growing up in Iran, I wondered why my father and mother left the comforts of life in America and a lucrative medical profession for living in Tabriz, laboring among a people who were so different in culture and for a mere fraction of the income. This question grew in intensity as I reached my teenage years. I recall sitting in the kitchen of the missionary house provided by the First Presbyterian Church of Lambertville, New Jersey. My parents were home on furlough and I finally got up the courage to confront my mother with the nagging question that had been bouncing around my head all that time.

She answered with the story of my father's birth.

My father's family had lived for three generations in Oxford, a fishing village in Talbert County, Maryland. To this day there is a street named Stewart Street and a Maryland Historic house called the Stewart House stands right next to the pier where the Tred-Avon Oxford-Bellevue Ferry docks. My great-grandfather was the county clerk, and his name is still inscribed on the cornerstone of the courthouse in Easton, MD. My great aunt was the first public school teacher there.

My father's birth was dramatic. He had been a twin, and the first child had been premature and stillborn. When my father was born, all were concerned that he would not survive. There were no incubators in those days, so the family called on another family member (whose name was never told to me) who had a reputation for having a strong faith and devoted prayer life. This family member came to the hospital and prayed over my father: "Dear God, if you save this child, we consecrate him to Afghanistan!" What seemed so strange about this prayer was that most of those who heard this prayer did not even know where Afghanistan was! Also, I wondered why he felt led to pray this way, other than it had been the leading of the Holy Spirit. But one thing became clear: God heard that prayer and my father thrived as a little baby and grew to be a very healthy man.

Apparently, my father's parents decided not to tell him about the prayer made over him at his birth. Perhaps they were fearful that he would feel some sort of rejection, thinking his parents were raising him only to send him to some distant land. Or maybe they feared that if they simply forgot about it, God would forget also and they would not have to lose their son to the mission field. God did not forget. My father, at a very early age, showed an unusual interest in Afghanistan and its people. When I was in seventh grade, our family was home on furlough from Iran and we stayed with my grandfather in the house in which my father had grown up. I remember seeing a scrapbook with my father's newspaper and magazine clippings from Afghanistan. I also know that I was born while my father was in military service in Germany, and when he returned to the States, he and my mother decided to apply for missionary service with the Board of Foreign Mission of the Presbyterian Church. He requested to be sent to Afghanistan and was deeply disappointed to learn that Afghanistan did not accept Christian missionaries. He was informed, however, that doctors were greatly needed in Iran, so he opted to go, claiming that it was "at least next door to Afghanistan."

I believe it is also noteworthy that my parents attended Tenth Presbyterian Church during the years that Dr. Donald Grey Barnhouse was the senior pastor. My mother was a student nurse at Hahnemann University Hospital while my father was studying at the University of Pennsylvania. Their dating consisted of attending the evening service at Tenth Presbyterian to hear Dr. Barnhouse preach. When my father brought up the topic of marriage, her primary concern was whether he, too, was called to the mission field? That was the criteria for her decision whether she should marry my father. My mother's sense of call was *that* strong. They were married in 1945; I was born in 1946 while my father was in Germany, and they departed for Iran in 1947.

After my heart-to-heart talk with my mother that day so long ago in Lambertville, New Jersey, I now knew why my father and mother had gone to Iran. God had filled their hearts with a passion for the Muslim world. My father's original call to Afghanistan was eventually fulfilled in his later years, as he was able to serve as a physiatrist equipping Afghan doctors in treating handicapped patients by developing prosthetics from materials found in the local bazaar. My mother ran the Mission guesthouse for traveling missionaries, providing them a clean place to stay for a minimal fee. She also served in the coffeehouse, "Del Aram" ("Peaceful Heart"), a ministry in Kabul, Afghanistan that grew out of a concern for all the American and European hippies who were on their way to India to find their "gurus." The foreign Christian community, under the leadership of Rev. Christy Wilson, saw an opportunity to share the love of Christ with the hippies who often arrived in Kabul hungry, penniless, and, all too often, sick. Del Aram became a place of food, shelter, and love. My mother spent many hours ministering to those wandering souls, and many heard the Gospel; eternity will reveal how many found faith in Christ because of that ministry.

Over the years, I have reflected much on how important it was for me to understand the dynamics of passion in their lives. I had the example of my parents who were passionately in love with Christ and whose hearts burned with zeal to serve Him in the Muslim world. Over the years of living with them and seeing their servant hearts, I also wanted to learn more about how God motivated them. I wondered if I too would ever have that burning desire for God and for His call upon my life. I decided to explore the role passion played in my own life and the lives of others.

The Power of Passion

"As a deer pants for the flowing streams, so pants my soul for you, O God. My soul thirsts for God, for the living God. When shall I come and appear before you?" ESV (Psalm 42:1-2)

What a picture of passion: thirsty deer, seeking with all their being to find water to quench their thirst. The psalmist equates what he observed about deer with his own thirst for God. Undoubtedly, the psalmist had lived in the wilderness and had studied the habits of deer. What he saw, if I could see also, would unlock the mystery of passion for me. Over time, as I studied this text, God showed me how to develop real-life passion for God in others.

The first principle I observed was that **the deer became passionate about what they needed most.** I knew of a young man named Ali, an only child who lived in southern Iran. His parents had died when he was a teenager, so he lived alone. He earned a living repairing radios and his nickname was "Ali-radio-ee." He loved to listen to the radio late at night and had felt especially drawn to the music playing on a Christian radio station. Over time, the music and the message of Christ began to penetrate his heart, and he longed to meet some Christians to find more answers to his many questions. To the best of his knowledge, there were no Christians that lived in his city in Iran, but he had heard there were Christians in Istanbul, Turkey. His longing to know more about Jesus was overpowering him. Because he had no family to tie him down, he sold his house and traveled to Istanbul.

As he wandered down Takseem Square in downtown Istanbul, he saw a cross over a building and became hopeful that he might finally meet some Christians. Imagine the hunger that drove him to knock on the door that, unbeknownst to him, led to a Catholic church. He was somehow able to make his desires known and was referred to a new membership class, where they informed him it would take at least two years to become a Christian. He was most likely given this impossible time frame to encourage him to leave, as the Catholic Church did not want to be accused of converting Muslims. But Ali was passionate and decided it would be worth two years of his life to get to know Jesus. After a few weeks of sitting in a class taught in Turkish, he realized that the real reason it would take two years was that he would first have to learn Turkish! He became extremely discouraged. But, as is often the case, God meets us in our darkest moments; one of his classmates suggested he attend the Iranian Church. Ali could hardly believe what he was hearing! An Iranian church? Was it possible? They gave him the address and he ran most of the way to the church. Unfortunately, it was Monday and there was no one there to welcome him. For the next few days, he kept an eye out, waiting for someone to show up. He wondered to himself why it was so hard to find someone who could tell him about Jesus. By the weekend, all the neighborhood children had gotten to know him, for he had spent the week playing soccer in the street with them and had purchased candy for them. When Sunday finally rolled around, the doors of the church opened and people began to gather. Again, he was disappointed because those who came to worship were Armenians; now he asked himself, "Do I have to learn Armenian to become a follower of Jesus?" With a downcast heart, he sat on the steps of the church, not sure what to do next. But then he heard a very sweet sound. It was the sound of people speaking Farsi! His heart swelled with hope. He saw a band of young Iranians, with one young man carrying a guitar. They greeted him warmly and invited him in. He followed them in like a little lost sheep. As the service began, he recognized some of the songs. Then the preacher talked about Jesus and Ali's heart became warmed to the message; when the pastor gave an invitation to come forward, Ali nearly knocked over a few people as he ran to the front to surrender his life to Jesus. Ali had finally found what he felt he needed the most, for it had become his passion.

A second principle that became evident was that **whatever one's passion is, is what will become preeminent.** That passion will override everything else. These thirsty deer had only one thing on their minds. They were not interested in anything other than finding the water that would quench their thirsts. Our deepest need is to know God, for He is the living water that can quench our spiritual thirst.

When I was a boy, I had not understood what my father's passion was, because my passion was to have nice clothes like the kids in America and to own a car. But that which was preeminent in my father's heart was to serve Christ. It would take many years before God would take hold of my heart and give me a passion for serving Christ and answering the call to serve the Persian-speaking world.

As I continued to meditate on the deer that are driven to find water to quench their thirst, the Lord showed me another important principle. **It is our passion that has the greatest influence on others.** We may think it is our words that deeply influence others or even our Christ-like life. Undoubtedly, those things do influence others. But if you are a thirsty deer and unable to detect the slightest scent of water, simply seeing a group of deer running wildly in one direction with resolve can capture your attention. It is only natural for the lost to follow others who know where they are going.

NO STRANGER

Naturally, my parents had a profound influence on me. But there was another man whose life intersected mine in many influential ways. His name was Dr. William M. Miller[3].

My first memory of Dr. Miller was just after my father was reassigned to the Christian Hospital in Mashhad, Iran, when I was about 13 years old. It was a big change for our family, who had made Tabriz our home for most of my young life. It was the first year I would go to a boarding school in Tehran, and my parents thought it would be better if I took the eighteen-hour train ride with an adult rather than traveling alone. When they heard that Dr. Miller would be traveling to Tehran about the same time, they planned for me to accompany him. Before the appointed day of travel, I went to see Dr. Miller to finalize the travel plans. Now, I had always gone first class on the train

Dr. William M. Miller

since it came with a bunk bed and air-conditioning, and only cost ten dollars. But to my surprise, Dr. Miller informed me we would not be going first-class. My mind instantly visualized what second-class would be like. No bunk bed, six to a compartment, and having to sit up all night. But before I could get over the shock of going second class, he added we would not be going second-class either, but he had made reservations for *third*-class. Now I was in full panic mode! How could I survive eighteen hours in a third-class train compartment with eight people sitting on wooden benches?

I suggested a counter proposal. "If it is a matter of the money, Dr. Miller, I am happy to come up with whatever it costs."

Dr. Miller laughed. "Tat, it is not a matter of the money, we *want* to go third class." I thought to myself, "Dr. Miller, *you* want to go third class." But I said nothing and prepared myself for what I knew was going to be a terrible train ride to Tehran.

The dreaded day arrived, and I climbed aboard the train. From the very beginning, I was miserable. It was hot and there were eight adults crammed into the third-class compartment. As the trip progressed, my attitude progressively got worse. But I noticed that Dr. Miller was having a wonderful time. He had learned the names of all of our fellow passengers

---

3. Dr. Miller's autobiography, <u>My Persian Pilgrimage</u>, can be found on Amazon.

who were graciously sharing their food with him. He was telling them stories from Jesus' life while I was praying for relief from my personal discomfort.

Finally, after a sleepless night on my part, we arrived in Tehran. Dr. Miller had become a friend to everyone, and every single one had accepted Gospel tracts from him. There were warm best wishes extended as we disembarked. I, on the other hand, was glad to be released from my night of torment, in contrast to Dr. Miller's sense of joy in sharing the gospel with a captive audience.

Years later, I reflected on my horrendous train ride and realized that Dr. Miller's passion was for God, and he lived to make the gospel known to the people of Iran. My passion, however, was for my own comfort and I wanted to travel through life thinking of what was best for me. But through this experience, Dr. Miller's enthusiasm had a deep influence on me.

These three questions would become a driving force in my life: *What was my deepest need? What or who was preeminent in my life?* And *what would be my greatest influence on the lives of others?* It would take time, but God would eventually lead me to find my own answers to these pressing questions.

CHAPTER TWO
EARLY INFLUENCES

    Growing up in Tabriz, I was exposed to many different worlds. First, there was the world of our home. We lived in a large house in the Tabriz Christian Hospital compound, surrounded by twelve-foot-high mud walls, which insulated us from being in contact with our neighbors. Yet each day, the outside world seeped into the hospital compound as patients lined up to take a number and wait their turn to see a doctor. From our front steps, I could often see the patients lining up, and often I would walk by them on my way to the main gate. We were always conscious of the hospital's presence, for that was where our father spent most of his time. And we, like everyone else, would stand in respect whenever he appeared and greet him with the words, "Salam Aghayeh Doctor" (Hello Mister Doctor). When there were emergencies at night, a frequent occurrence, we were awakened by an orderly knocking on our door to inform my father he was needed. My father later told me how rewarding it was to practice medicine in Tabriz because they had actual diseases for which modern medicine most often had a treatment or a cure. He contrasted that with practicing medicine in the west where there were many more incidents of psychosomatic illnesses. (My daughter has written a fascinating book on this topic, coincidentally.) [4] My father faced many medical challenges, however, and I remember watching him eating his lunch and reviewing the steps of the surgery he would have to perform that afternoon. Having a mother as a nurse and a father as a doctor, I suppose, could have led me to pursue a career in medicine. Although such a decision might have overjoyed my father, I had seen enough illness and

---

4. <u>Hiding: What Fig Leaves and Chronic Pain Have in Common</u> by Emily Stewart, available on Amazon.

disease to know I wanted to follow a different path. However, my parents instilled in me a desire to serve others for Christ's sake, whether it was in meeting their physical or their spiritual needs, and for that, I am forever grateful.

Since there were no English-language schools in Tabriz, my mother had to homeschool us. We had a special room designated for school in our home and every morning all year round, my mother taught us. She preferred teaching us half days so she could do ministry in the afternoons. She loved leading Bible studies for the women employees of the hospital and teaching English to Iranian university students. She had one rule for her students, and that was that the Gospel of Mark be their text. Only Heaven knows how many of her students came to faith in Christ by being exposed to her kindness and the Word of God. She spent a good part of our class period teaching us the Bible, along with teaching us the great hymns of the church. She would often say, "I really do not care what profession you choose as long as you serve Jesus."

Tabriz Christian Hospital

My world changed as our family grew. My brother Lennie was born and soon my first sister, Peggie, arrived, followed by another brother, Billy. Years later, my parents had two more children, Louise and Ruth. We were three boys and three girls. We were all taught to love God's Word and to love Christ and each other. I have many wonderful memories of life together in the big house in Tabriz. I later learned that my mother prayed that all six of her children would serve God on a different continent. Up to this point, we have served on four. Just as my father modeled service, my mother modeled a deep devotion to the Word of God. Every morning I came down to the dining room for breakfast to find her sitting at the dining room table with her open Bible alongside a notebook in which she was taking notes. She especially loved the Psalms and she read through Charles Spurgeon's commentaries on the Psalms more than once. I later learned from her that she had pored over the Scriptures looking for promises that God makes for children and claimed every one she found for her own children. My mother loved Jesus and taught me to do the same. Years later, when I was serving as pastor of the Church of the Atonement in Silver Spring, Maryland, and my parents were living in Kabul, Afghanistan, she wrote to tell me, "Each

Saturday, I pray that when you enter the pulpit to preach on Sunday, you will experience the joy of the Lord." How wonderful it was to know that she was in prayer for me. Her life was and, although she has been gone now for ten years, still is a dominant influence in my devotion to Christ.

The second world I was exposed to was the Azeri culture of Tabriz. As I grew old enough to have friends my age, I quickly learned to speak Azeri. In fact, to this day, I often speak it with my brother. Growing up in Tabriz has left a lasting mark on me. For example, when I speak Farsi, there is a residue of an Azeri accent that causes some Iranian friends to laugh, for it is quite a unique thing to hear an American speaking Farsi with an Azeri accent! Being able to speak Azeri has also given me a special bond with millions of people who live in Iran and who love to hear their mother tongue. To this day, I am often asked to deliver New Year's greetings in Azeri on Christian satellite programs.

Along with the new language I had to learn, I was exposed to a new culture that was steeped in the religion of Islam. Islam permeated my life. Many employees of the hospital were Muslims, and I witnessed their fasting during the month of Ramadan. During the month of Moharam, there were celebrations commemorating the split that occurred after the Prophet Mohammad's death in 632 AD. There had been a conflict over how his successor would be chosen; some (the Sunnis) felt the choice should be made by the will of his followers, and others (the Shiites) felt that Ali, Mohammad's cousin and son-in-law, was the obvious heir chosen by God. In 680 AD, in the Battle of Karbala, Ali's grandsons, Hussein and Hassan, were murdered. To this day, the Shiite Muslims of Iran spend the month of Moharam in public mourning and reenacting the events of Karbala. These noisy reenactments of the martyrdoms of Hussein and Hassan lasted into the night and kept me awake.

Through witnessing these Muslim customs, I realized the fear that gripped the hearts of many who did not know of the grace and mercy of God and thus lived in constant fear of an angry God. Perhaps God was preparing my heart to preach the Gospel someday to the people of Iran, as I saw with my own eyes the bondage of living in the darkness with multiple superstitions and rituals as their only hope.

One way I learned about what Muslims believed was through our gardener. One day, I noticed that Baghban (Gardener) Ali was chopping wood behind our house and tossing it into our basement for use during the winter months. It was a hot day during the month of Ramadan. I went out to keep him company and found a comfortable spot on a pile of wood to sit on. I began talking to him, and at one point, I asked him what he knew about Jesus and if he believed in Him.

His response surprised me. "We love Jesus more than you Christians do!" Then he schooled me on Islam. He told me that for Muslims, Jesus was one of the greatest of prophets and that they would never say he died on a cross because that would be too disrespectful. "We believe someone who looked like Jesus died on the cross, not Jesus himself," he continued. "Jesus was a prophet for his time, but Islam was the better religion since it was a later revelation given to humankind through the Prophet Mohammad." As he shared with me, I realized I had not been fully aware of what Muslims believed about Jesus. Later, as I mulled over what Baghban Ali had taught me about Islam, it dawned on me how his religion basically denied who Jesus was – it upset me that my dear friend did not believe Jesus died on a cross for his sins.

On another occasion during the month of Ramadan, when Baghban Ali was daylight fasting, I got up enough courage to ask him why he fasted. I said, "It must be very hard to work all day when you have not eaten." He agreed and explained that he did it to please God, hoping God would accept him. Then I noticed that on his cleanly shaven head, there were four or five scars. I asked him, "Where did your scars come from?" I had heard that on the last day of Moharam, certain groups of Muslims went to the cemetery and slashed their heads with sharp knives to share in the suffering of the prophet Ali's martyrdom. But I had never had a chance to ask someone directly about this practice. His answer was not very clear to me, but I understood that he thought that, by his own suffering, he could appease God's wrath for his sins. I was only eight or nine years old but my heart was distressed to think of my friend Ali the gardener slashing his head with a sharp knife hoping to pay for his sins by sharing in the suffering of a dead prophet. But what I discovered in sharing with Baghban Ali about Jesus was that my words seemed to make no difference to him. I was merely a child, and he had lived a lifetime believing in the teaching of Islam.

I am certain that God planned all these experiences for me as he was preparing me to be His servant someday to bring the Good News of the gospel to the people of Iran. I learned that when a person has a close Muslim friend, the burden for their salvation becomes intensified, and it is in friendship that the gospel is best shared. As one of my mentors expressed it, "First, make a heart connection before you try to make a gospel connection." The Afghans have a great saying: "I will not follow my enemy to Heaven, but I will follow my friend to Hell." I learned it is the Holy Spirit who opens the hearts of Muslims.

"What no eye has seen, nor ear heard, nor the heart of man imagined what God has prepared for those who love him, these things God has revealed to us through the Spirit." (I Corinthians 2:9 -10) This truth has guided me over a lifetime of sharing the gospel with Muslims. God saves! But I must be bold and find ways to share. First, my life has to have the aroma of Christ by demonstrating kingdom of God realities. Second, I must be prepared to answer the many questions that Muslims have. Third, I need to be a good apologist and be able to give a reason for the faith that I have. Those conversations I had in Tabriz so many years ago were the beginnings of my preparations for how to live and minister the truth to my Muslims friends. I believe I planted some seeds in Baghban Ali's heart that I trust God watered, and I could only pray that God saved his soul.

As much as Islam colored my world, there were other aspects of life in Tabriz that were wonderful. It introduced me to the world of honor and shame. My father, as a doctor and the director of the Tabriz Hospital, was always addressed as "Aghahyeh Doctor Stewart" (Mister Doctor Stewart). This was so impressed upon me that I often referred to my father as "Aghahyeh Doctor." And I soon learned that the respect given to my father was also extended to me as his son. When I went to the local corner store, the owner stood to welcome me as Aghahyeh Doctor Stewart's son. That made me feel important and honored, and I learned how important it was to show respect to others, particularly those who were older.

I also witnessed how an honor culture translates into hospitality. We were often invited to the homes of Iranians, which was always a treat for a growing boy who loved to eat. Guests were treated as if they were family. One example of this generosity was Khadijeh, the woman who did our weekly wash by hand. She was her family's breadwinner, since her husband, Gholi, was handicapped with Parkinson's disease. They had two boys about the same ages as my brother Lennie and I, Nasser and Houshang. Their father often came to the hospital compound to take us the almost hour-long trek to their home. They lived in one of the poorest neighborhoods in Tabriz; their home was a one-room house with a small hallway and a tiny kitchen. They had a little pool with one spigot of water for the entire house, along with an old-fashioned outhouse. In the winter, they heated their home as many poor people did, with a large table covered by a large quilt ("kursi"), under which would be a small pit filled with burning charcoal. Large, firm pillows surrounded the table, offering support and comfort. The family sat in a circle around the table and placed their legs under the quilt to stay warm. Some families slept there all night. Going to their home was God's exposing me to what it was like to be poor and to see how hard life was for them. Yet it also showed me that being poor did not mean one had to be poor in outlook or attitude. This family welcomed my brother and me with open arms. In the summer, we cooled off in their little pool ("hoze") and in the winter we slipped under the quilt to get warm as they served us hot tea.

Tabriz hospitality was amazing and was most on display during the two weeks of NoRuz (Iranian New Year celebration around March 21st). During these two weeks, people held open houses for friends to drop in to wish them blessings for the New Year, and then would themselves visit their friends' homes, so everyone was busy making the rounds. It was therefore expected that my parents would bring us along to visit all the hospital employees, so we all climbed into a horse and buggy to visit several homes each day.

One particular NoRuz stands out. Our family was going to visit Khadijeh and Gholi, but when we arrived in a horse and buggy, it caused quite a stir in the neighborhood. The family greeted us warmly, standing at the little gate to their yard. As we made our way into their one-room house, I noticed the walls had been freshly painted, the warm carpets were spotless, and there were two straight-backed chairs placed at the head of the room. They escorted my parents to the chairs. I thought little about it, as the sweets and fruit that were on the table before us distracted me. But on the way home, my mother explained how touched she and my father had been because Gholi had rented those two chairs for them so that they would not have to sit on the floor, as was the custom. She told me he had spent a day's wages to honor them and make them comfortable in their home. It was experiences such as this that helped me find deep appreciation and respect for the people of Tabriz and their strong family ties. God used Gholi and his family to help shape the person I am today by their honoring our family.

I have shared how my life was shaped by the world of our home and by the world of the Azeri Turkish culture. But in all this, there was another vital influence on my early life — the Turkish Church. Church was always a big part of my parents' lives and we were always expected to go to church with them. There was no debate or question about going to church, no matter the weather. Every

The "Big House"/Stewart Home in Tabriz

Sunday I had to dress up in my "Made in Tabriz" wool suit that my mother had had specially made for me. I hated wearing it since it was so scratchy that I would have to wear my pajama bottoms under them. Then we would wait for the horse and buggy to enter the hospital compound and come park in front of the big house. We always began our journey down Shahnaz Avenue, across Pahlavi Avenue, and after winding our way through several alleys, we arrived in front of the gates of the church. There our driver, whose name was "Uzum," waited for us until church was over.

One Sunday after church, I came out of the church gate and climbed into the carriage to wait for my parents. Just then I heard loud shouting as the narrow alley swelled with young men shouting "Yankee, go home!" I was stunned, never having had experienced such disdain from anyone in Tabriz.

I felt hurt and insulted, and thought to myself, "I am a Tabrizi also; why do you want me to leave?" Later, my father explained to me about what was happening politically and told me about Mr. Mosaddegh and how he was trying to free Iran from western powers controlling the Iranian oil industry.

Mohammad Mosaddegh became the 35th Prime minister of Iran in 1951. His major accomplishment was nationalizing the Iranian oil industry, which had been built by the British who had controlled the Iranian oil industry since 1913. His government was overthrown because he tried to dissolve Parliament and give himself and his cabinet complete power, thus stripping the King ("Shah") of his power. In a now infamous covert military operation known as "Operation Ajax" (referred to as "the Coup" in Farsi) British and American intelligence services, with Iranian support, used rogue elements in the military and removed Mosaddegh from office on Aug. 19, 1953 (28 Mordad 1332). After the Coup he was court-martialed and sentenced to three years in prison. In an illegal move, even by the regime's own standards, the Shah's government exiled him to house arrest in a remote village owned by his family until his death on March 5, 1967. They laid him to rest inside the dining room of his residence in the village of Ahmadabad in a private ceremony.

Stewart Family Riding to Church

Emotionally, I found myself on the side of Iran, but it also occurred to me that I was an American living as a guest in Iran, which produced in me a realization that in some strange way I had dual identities. That day left me somewhat confused, for living as a minority in a foreign land can make one wonder where he really belonged. Perhaps my experience of growing up as a foreigner in Iran provided me with more sensitivity when later in life I served Iranians living in America.

Once in church, I was immersed in yet another world: the world of Evangelical[5] Christians who came from several different ethnic backgrounds. There were many Assyrians, like the Lazaar family, who were influential leaders in the church. There were Armenians who also played a large role in

---

5. Presbyterian Christians, also referred to as Injili.

leading the church, like Biran Hyrik, who was an interpreter at the American Consulate yet who often preached at our Turkish worship services. We sang hymns of praise in Turkish and heard the Word of God read and proclaimed in Turkish. The women sat on one side of the sanctuary and the men on the other. Children sat with their parents until they were old enough to sit by themselves. I cannot remember how many hundreds of sermons I listened to, but I remember the love and kindness that I experienced in that church. Miss Wooding, who was headmistress of the Mission Nursing School, often played the organ, powered by leg power. I can still see her legs pumping away as her fingers glided over the keyboard. It is funny to think of the little things such as her wearing her glasses upside down as she played the organ.

Most of the church consisted of traditionally Christian ethnic groups, but there were a few Muslim converts, one of whom, Asad, I befriended as a boy. He was a blind man who had been raised by a German ministry for the blind. I loved seeing him coming and would happily take his hand to lead him to his seat on the front row. Then I sat by him. There were several things that intrigued me about him. Halfway through every sermon, he would take out his Braille watch to gauge when the sermon would end. I looked forward to this time because it gave me hope that the sermon was almost over. But the thing that touched my young heart the most was how he seemed to know all the hymns by heart and how he belted them out with such passion. I saw his clouded eyes, and it was as though he could see something that I could not. He undoubtedly had spiritual sight. He has remained in my memory all these years as a vivid reminder to me that without the regenerating power of the Holy Spirit, one cannot really perceive one's sinful state and need for the forgiveness that God offers us through Jesus. I praise God that when I was six years old, I committed my life to Christ as the Holy Spirit used my Mom to open my eyes to see the truth as well.

There was another lady from a Muslim background in the church in Tabriz, whom my mother had befriended. She had come to faith in Christ as a teenager. She always came to church in a chador (a usually black head-to-toe cloth covering worn by Shiite Muslim women, usually black; women never left their homes without wearing one). I also remember her bright reddish hair dyed with "Henna" (a reddish dye used to color hair or beards and to paint temporary hand tattoos, considered beneficial for the hair and scalp in preventing premature graying and reducing dandruff). My mother often helped her financially and visited her regularly. My mother told me that since she had given her life to Christ, her family had completely disowned her because she was now considered unclean so no one would marry her. She lived in a one-room apartment that the church paid for, and she depended on gifts that church members brought her. Seeing her every Sunday in church opened my eyes to the price many Muslim converts pay for being disciples of Christ. It helped me understand why many Muslims who hear the gospel either become secret followers of Jesus or reject Him out of fear. The courage that I saw in this lady left a deep impression on me, and when I see what my Iranian and Afghan brothers and sisters suffer for the sake of Christ, I am still inspired to press on in my own life to be more courageous in my witness for Christ.

The Tabriz church was not a place of peace and joy for all who attended. There was a nurse from our nursing school who was from a Muslim background who had become a Christian at the cost of losing her family. The problem she faced was that there were those in the church from non-Muslim backgrounds who could not accept her as a genuine believer. There may have been many reasons for that. For one, she may have retained behaviors from her previous life that carried over and troubled the believers. But there was also a deep suspicion among the Armenian and Assyrian believers because of the many ways they had experienced persecution from Muslims throughout their history. Whatever the reasons, her former family had rejected our sister Kokab and now she did not feel accepted by her new family, which left her in a hard place emotionally. The missionaries tried to fill the gap, but the sad consequence was that Kokab eventually tried to take her own life. I remember hearing my parents discussing this issue in low tones. I had never heard of anyone trying to kill themselves before, and could not imagine why anyone would do that. But knowing Kokab and learning of her inner struggles with depression because of rejection was God's way of preparing me for the genuine struggles that Muslim converts often face. It has helped me to be less judgmental and more caring and supportive of those who have paid a great price to follow the Master, who gave His life for them.

My overall impression of the Evangelical Church in Tabriz in those years long before the Islamic Revolution was that it was very traditional, with little change from week to week. There was a quiet, steady faith that most seemed to have, but there did not seem to be much evangelism going on. I never recall seeing an adult baptism, which would have been evidence of a new convert. Little did we know then that after the Islamic revolution, this sleepy little church would become a haven for many new believers. Years later, I had the privilege of meeting the man who pastored the Tabriz church in the year after the Revolution. He was a humble man who was arrested and sent to prison for a time for his faith. I remember his telling me how he had shepherded his flock during those days. Muslim background believers were prohibited from attending the services in the church sanctuary, so he visited them one by one during the course of a week. He met some of them at certain locations in the city and walked with them for a while. He shared his sermon of the week with them and prayed with them. By using this method given to him by the Holy Spirit, he was able to keep in touch with his flock.

Evangelical Church in Tabriz

God uses persecution upon his church to drive believers to seek Him. However, persecution also scatters and grows the church as believers seek relief. Winds of persecution carry the seeds of the gospel further than during any time of peace and prosperity. As I witnessed these truths in the church of Iran, I gained a much deeper confidence in the sovereignty of God and became even more encouraged having taken part in the story of God's wonderful work in Iran.

CHAPTER THREE
MASHHAD

Life has a way of lulling one into passivity, but God has a way of awakening us to new experiences that deepen our dependence on Him. I was a quite happy 12-year-old growing up in Tabriz. I had learned Turkish well enough to enjoy my relationships with my Iranian friends, many who were Muslims. I also had a number of Armenian friends whose mothers worked as housekeepers for the missionary families, so I learned Armenian as well. My school schedule was flexible; I had every afternoon off to play in the large compound that was my kingdom. My family was growing and now I had brothers and sisters — Lennie, Peggie and Billy — to play with, or even to press them into serving my wishes (as they have often reminded me). Life seemed very good!

Then came the news that rocked my world. I couldn't believe it! How could my parents go along with it?

The Mission that oversaw the six Christian hospitals in Iran had decided to transfer my father to the city of Mashhad. Where was Mashhad anyway? Why would they do this?

I learned that Dr. and Mrs. Thomas Murray's family would be going on furlough, and they needed my father to become the director of the Christian Hospital of Mashhad while they were away. As much as my parents tried to assure me it was not the end of the world, I saw it as a complete downgrade.

The process of moving was complicated. Our houseful of furniture had to be crated so that the long, arduous trip of almost a thousand miles by truck would not destroy them. We packed our personal belongings and took the train ride to Tehran and then on to Mashhad in the northwestern corner of Iran. We arrived there on March 3rd, my brother Lennie's birthday. The

Murray family greeted us enthusiastically. Who knew that one day, their daughter, Patty, would become my bride? At that point, however, I was most impressed with her mother, Nancy, who insisted on celebrating Lennie's birthday by baking a cake. We gathered later that day at the Murray home for a memorable celebration.

Mashhad differed greatly from Tabriz. The gardens where we lived were bursting with beautiful flowers and fruit trees. It seemed like some kind of paradise to me. Each missionary family had their own walled-in yard with connecting gates. Each yard had a resident gardener (a "baghban") who lived onsite with their families, and their children became our new friends. The first challenge I faced was the fact that everyone spoke Farsi and I, having lived in Tabriz, spoke only Turkish. But to my delight, our gardener, "Moslem," spoke Azeri, as did his two sons. So, their family became my best friends and to this day I have maintained contact with them. Our gardener was a kind and gentle man. He took it upon himself to give me guidance on many topics. I sometimes went shopping with him and he showed me where the best shops were. He told me to stand up straight since I had a tendency to be hunched over because of my height of nearly 6'4". He welcomed me often into their one-room house for tea and an occasional meal.

Tat Buying Homing Pigeons With Friend Moslem

God used him to teach me about life in Iran and to help me better understand the Iranian culture.

While living in Mashhad, I discovered the fine art of raising homing pigeons. As kids, we had many different animals living in our yard: dogs, cats, chicken and even sheep. But I was first introduced to the underworld of homing pigeons in Mashhad. With the help of the gardener's boys, we had to first prepare a room that had been formerly used for keeping plants safe during the winter months. Using bricks and small boards, we built some pigeon holes that could serve as nests. Then came the question of where to purchase healthy birds? I was advised to look for a man who was called

Hadji. Accompanied by some Iranian friends, we found Mr. Hadji who lived in a room overlooking Imam Reza's shrine. His room was filthy since he lived with his pigeons. We bought a pair of good healthy pigeons, which we were assured would be good for breeding, and left as quickly as we could. We clipped the wings of the pigeons so they would not fly home to their previous owner and waited for them to mate and produce baby pigeons, or "squabs." With the help of my friends, we grew my flock to over twenty pigeons, which we flew twice a day. I looked forward each day to the time I could watch my flock soaring high in the sky, swirling around and around. Some of my pigeons climbed far above the rest of the flock and would then drop back down doing somersaults. Then the ultimate thrill came when I called them back with a whistle and scattered seed on the ground. I will never forget the joy I felt during that time!

Lessons From Pigeons

I learned many lessons from raising pigeons that, oddly enough, helped me when I eventually became a pastor. While people are, of course, far more complex than birds, my experience in training pigeons helped me to become more creative in motivating a diverse flock to become unified under my leadership:

Pigeons are very loyal to their home and owner. As I soon learned with the first pair of pigeons I purchased, I had to clip their wings so that they would not fly back to their old home. I could not let them fly again until they had produced two squabs. Once they had young ones to feed they stayed with me. When people have invested in something, they show more loyalty.

Pigeons are best trained to fly when they are hungry. I let mine fly around my rooftop and as soon as they were in the air, I scattered seeds on the roof and they would descend rapidly to eat. Leading them with a trail of seeds, I would then lure them back into their cage. I repeated this for days and as time went by, they would fly longer and higher but would always come back when I scattered seed on the roof. When people are fed, they keep coming back.

When they flew, they flew as a flock. This was to help keep them all together so that they would all safely land again on my roof. If a pigeon went out on its own, another person's flock could swallow it up and I might lose it. The reverse was also possible; my flock could surround a stray pigeon and bring it back to me. This was the game that pigeon raisers played and they even made money on it as they might sell back the pigeon that they had captured. Unity is essential for the safety of the group.

As time went by, I learned the personalities of my pigeons. Some were show-offs and liked to tumble and do somersaults in the air. Others were bullies and pushed others around. Some were jealous and tried to get more attention. But when they flew, they were all together as one flock and they all came home to me, their owner. People have unique challenges and gifts that need to be addressed individually for the group to thrive.

Mashhad is known for its fabulous fruit! There is nothing quite like a bowl of dark red Bing cherries from Mashhad. The garden we lived in had many fruit trees and my friends and I watched each tree in anticipation of when the fruit would ripen. One of the large trees in our yard was a "Shahtoot" tree (mulberry). I have seen nothing quite like it anywhere else. When the berries, or "toots", were ripe, they became plump, dark red juicy mulberries. My mother noticed the ripe berries and admonished me not to eat any. Her reasoning was, "If you start, you will eat too many and that could give you a stomachache." An hour later, when she had gone shopping, my friends knocked on our door. As I greeted them, they said excitedly, "The toots are ripe and they are calling us!" I hung my head to show my regrets that I would not be joining them. I had to admit what every young person never wants to have to tell his friends: "My mom said no." They looked at me with that look that said, *Are you serious?* "Your mother is not home, so she will never know." If you are going to sin, it is always comforting to know that everyone else is going along with you. So I slipped out of our front door and climbed up in the large welcoming branches of the "toot" tree. How can I ever describe what that first "toot" tasted like? It was better than I had ever imagined. Before I knew it, I was downing them as fast as I could. The juice was dripping down my arms and a dark red ring was taking shape around my mouth. Sin can really taste good at first. But the inevitable happened. My mother returned sooner than I had expected. Perched high in the old tree, I could see her coming. I slid down that tree faster than a fireman slides down his pole on his way to a fire. I ran into the kitchen, looked for the lye soap that was often used for washing rugs, and scrubbed my hands and face as hard and as fast as I could. But to my great dismay, every time I looked in the mirror, the stains remained and after all the rubbing my face and hands seemed even redder. Finally, after what seemed like an eternity, the front door opened and there I stood with the evidence of my sin written all over my face. Needless to say, my mother was not happy at all. I was strongly rebuked for my disobedience and sent to my room. That evening, after I had been sufficiently punished, I stepped outside to see how my friends had fared. The first thing I noticed about them was that their stains were gone. I told them my sad story and then curiosity got the best of me and I asked them why they did not have any stains. That's when they shared the secret of getting rid of "toot" stains. Every Iranian knows, but I had to learn the hard way: take the leaves of the "toot" tree and crush them — the sap in the leaves is the only thing that can take the stain away! I must admit I was pretty angry with them for not educating me before I got punished for eating the forbidden fruit. This experience has become a favorite story for me, and I have used it often in explaining the gospel to Iranians.

Mashhad is one of the holiest cities for the Shiite Muslims of Iran because it is where the shrine of Imam Reza is located. Thousands of pilgrims — women who can't get pregnant, those suffering from rare illnesses, and those simply looking for God to give them good fortune — annually visit the shrine hoping to get special favors from God. When one arrives in Mashhad, one of the first things that catches the eye is the gold-plated dome of Imam Reza's shrine sparkling in the sunlight. It must be a deeply inspiring sight for the pilgrims who flock there every year. It was in this sacred city for Muslims that I lived and learned more about Islam. Not only was I gaining more exposure to the culture of Islam through Muslim friends, I was learning how deeply Muslims believed that they personally could not have a relationship with God so they had to find "holy" men to be their intermediaries between them and God.

On one occasion, our gardener Moslem, whom I loved very much since he had adopted me like a son, invited me to take a walk around the great Imam Reza Mosque that housed his tomb. I had been asking him many questions about what he believed, and he was patient to answer them. He later suggested that we could visit the shrine, and I accepted his invitation. To prepare for our visit to the shrine, he informed me I should wear some older clothes, take off my glasses (few Iranians wore glasses in those days), and speak only Turkish. The appointed day arrived, and I was filled with mixed emotions since my friends had told me that if it was discovered that I was a Christian, I could be killed. I do not know how true that was, but I was determined not to say anything that might give me away. As we blended in with the throngs of pilgrims as they pressed toward Imam Reza's tomb, I noticed how people were kissing the tomb and prostrating themselves before it. A deep sense of sadness came over me as I observed the obvious idol worship and the despair in the people around me. I wanted to run away and get away from there as fast as I could. I determined never to go back, but I felt sorry for all these people who did not know what I knew, even as a young boy, about the grace of God and the freedom that the gospel brings. Was God placing a burden on my heart for the people of Iran? I did not realize how God was training me through my life for the call to minister to the Persian-speaking world. I compare my life to a plush, colorful Persian carpet. When it is on the loom, you can watch the weaver working, but the patterns have not yet become apparent. The weaver has already determined the pattern, but it is not yet obvious to the onlooker until the last threads have fallen into place.

In stark contrast to my time at Imam Reza's shrine, there was the wonderful Christian fellowship that I found in the youth group of the Injili (Evangelical) church in Mashhad. Whereas in Tabriz most of the youth were from Armenian or Assyrian heritage, where being a Christian was the norm, the youth group in Mashhad was made up of those from Muslim backgrounds. And because many of them lived in the hospital compound, we spent many hours a week together doing fun activities. A very famous landmark in Mashhad is Kooh-Sangi, which means Stone Mountain. It was about five miles from the hospital, but we got up early in the morning, packed a breakfast, and rode our bikes to Kooh-Sangi. We sat on the big rock to eat our breakfast and told jokes and laughed until our sides hurt.

I remember when all the boys in the youth group went camping.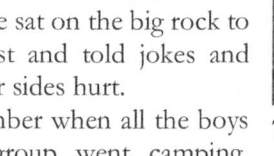

Tat with the Mashhad Youth

There is a very scenic valley called Akhlemad and one summer with our youth leader we hiked up the steep trail to a beautiful meadow where we pitched our tents and spent several nights. We sat out under the stars and talked about our faith in God and shared our dreams for life. We cooked our food over open fires and washed our faces in the cold brook that ran through the meadow. For those days we were together, we forgot about all the things that might have been troubling in our lives and celebrated our brotherhood in Christ.

The Mashhad church seemed to be to be very different from the church in Tabriz. To me, it seemed to be more alive, which may have been because I was older and I was surrounded by a lively youth group and deeper Christian leaders. We attended a weekly Bible study in Farsi, which was taught by different leaders. One time, when Dr. William Miller was visiting Mashhad, he took the time to lead one of our Bible studies. I remember his kind face and his deep convictions regarding the Word of God. Everyone had the greatest respect for him.

Our youth leaders also challenged us to care about the poor. One spring we planted a large vegetable garden with the purpose of giving the produce to poor families. I remember the long hours we spent toiling under the burning sun as we tended to our garden. It was a great experience of teamwork and was an excellent lesson for me in how to share in a selfless project since we saved none of the produce for ourselves.

The Mashhad church had some wonderful traditions. There were few new converts, but when there were, they often chose to be baptized on Easter Sunday. Being baptized on Easter in and of itself would have been a glorious way to celebrate the sacrament of baptism, but there was another motivation for the choice. Those who were to be baptized on Easter morning had a tradition of staying in the church from Good Friday until Easter morning. They would have a Bible study, sing hymns, and even fast for part of the time. The church made this time very special. Then, when Easter morning arrived, the entire church gathered for a sunrise service. I remember so well those Easter mornings. After a time of worship, we would gather and have a delicious Persian breakfast of hard-boiled eggs, fresh Persian bread, and freshly brewed tea. There was always such a wonderful spirit as we celebrated Christ's triumph over sin and death in His glorious resurrection by witnessing those new believers being baptized, after being, in a sense, "buried" in the church for three days.

Years later, when I served as a pastor of a Persian congregation, I came to better realize the wisdom of the three-night stay inside the church. What I discovered was that during the days leading up to the baptism of a Muslim convert, they usually came under great attack from the enemy. Some had nightmares; fear and doubts overcame others. Some did not even show up for their baptism because of these attacks from the enemy. Knowing this, the elders of the Mashhad church surrounded these men and women to protect them. They pastorally cared for their flock in a most loving and wise way. I learned from their example to prepare new believers for their baptism and the attacks that most likely would come in the pre-baptism days. We are engaged in a cosmic spiritual battle, and those who do not recognize it will most likely be hurt and discouraged.

Mashhad will always hold a special place in my heart. I had my first memories of seeing Patty Murray, whom I would later marry. I was introduced to her family, who in later years became very dear to me. Patty's father was deeply loved by his patients and the hospital staff. In fact, a young man who grew up in the hospital compound went to college and then to medical school with the help of the Murray family. Years after the Murrays had left Mashhad, he planned to erect a statue of Dr. Murray and place in a major thoroughfare. Others said that when Dr. Murray came into their hospital room, his radiant face made him look like an angel. He was deeply admired. Mrs. Murray also was deeply loved for her kindness and hospitality. I remember talking to one of the boys on the hospital compound and asking him what was it that drew him to Jesus? With no hesitation, he announced, "It was Mrs. Murray!" Then he told me why: Mrs. Murray was hosting a grand outdoor party where she had several tables set up in the yard, covered with white tablecloths. As the guests arrived, Mrs. Murray appeared in a white dress to welcome them. He paused as if to indicate, *Now here comes the important part of the story.* He said, "Another boy and I climbed up into a tree in the adjacent yard to get a better view of the festivities." The tree they climbed was a toot tree with big ripe mulberries dripping with red juice. With a very sheepish look on his face, he told me what happened next. "I really don't know why I did this, but my friend and I both started throwing toots onto the white tablecloths. As if that was not bad enough, I threw one that splattered onto the back of Mrs. Murray's white dress. At that point, some guests turned to look up in our direction, so we dropped to the ground as fast as we could and ran back to our homes and hid. That night I could not even sleep for fear that Mrs. Murray would show up at my

Murray Family 1957

doorstep and tell my parents what I had done. I was certain my father would be fired. The next morning, I saw Mrs. Murray walking towards our little house. It seemed the inevitable was about to happen. We heard her knock on the door and I reluctantly opened it. She announced with a big smile on her face that she had lots of leftover food from her party and she wanted to share it with my family. To this day, I know she knew it was I who had almost ruined her party, but she never mentioned it. That was a day I never forgot, for it was the first time I think that I first understood grace. I deserved condemnation for what I had done, but instead, I was invited to share in the delicious food from her party!"

I never forgot hearing this story about my future mother-in-law. And not only have I shared this story in many sermons I preached on grace, I too became the recipient of her love and grace for many years. I miss them both for never was a man as blessed as I was to have them as my in-laws.

CHAPTER FOUR
LIFE IN TEHRAN

The decision had been made in the highest courts of my family. No one asked me for my advice or opinion. I was now entering sixth grade, and it was time for me to go to a proper school in Tehran. The mission had just commissioned the construction of a boarding house and had appointed a missionary family to oversee it. I suppose my mother was ready to turn me over to professional teachers who might help me. You see, I had reached sixth grade and still could not read with any kind of comprehension.

I realized much later in my life just how much my mother had suffered in trying to educate me. As each school year passed, she wondered if it was her fault that I could not learn to read or if I was just dumb. Maybe there was something wrong with me she just could not figure out. Every time a visiting teacher would come to our home, my mother would consult with them for any way they might help me. Not only could I not read, but my writing was also pathetic. Now, for all those who might have had similar problems in learning, I must point out that in those days, no one knew about learning disabilities. There were no special classes or resources, so if a child had a problem, it was assumed he or she had a very low IQ or that they were lazy and unmotivated.

Years later, it was discovered that I was dyslexic, which meant that I often did not even see some words on the page and often reversed numbers. For example, the number 79 might look to me like 97. This was a real problem in dialing phone numbers. I often talked to people I had not intended to call! In doing my own research, I discovered people learn in different ways. For example, some learn through reading, thus learning visually. Some learn by watching how things work, so YouTube videos help them a lot. Others like me learn better by hearing. If I heard a story I could remember it, but if I read it, it did not make sense. My learning disability was actually a gift because it helped me learn two languages other than English; I learned both Azeri and Farsi simply by immersion. I studied Farsi formally for only a year, but I could quickly speak fluently.

My mother soon realized that I could not read books, so she read them to us as children. Growing up in Tabriz, we did not have many forms of entertainment. We had a yard filled with pets: dogs, cats, chickens, even an occasional turkey. We enjoyed riding bikes, and I had a wonderful wagon that my dad had specially made for me. Later, he even had skis made for Lennie and me. But once evening came there was not much to do, so my mother read many of the classics to us. We all gathered around as she read to us; that was our entertainment.

Given all my educational challenges, I can only assume that my mother and father reached the decision that, if there was going to be any hope for me, it would have to be in a formal school setting with professional teachers. So, they prepared Lennie and me to go to the boarding school in Tehran. I do not remember saying goodbye to them or the trip itself. But I remember how hard it was to adjust to life in the boarding house!

The first challenge was that it was very hot in Tehran in September. Mashhad had had cool evenings and the days were not as hot; not so in Tehran. Lennie and I were roommates, which would have been fine with me except for the fact that he was so homesick he cried every night. After all, he was only a fifth grader! I remember pleading with him not to cry, since that only made me cry, too! The longing for our parents and our home was overwhelming at times. Having to get up at a certain time every morning for room inspection before going off to school was a jarring experience for us at such a young age. I hated school and lived in constant anxiety. On the first day of school, they asked me to write my name on a form that the teacher handed out. I simply wrote: "Tat." When the form was returned to me, my teacher had written that I needed to include my last name as well. It was then that I realized I did not know how to spell my last name. I had been homeschooled all my life, so putting my first name on my papers was always enough. When other kids discovered I could not spell my last name, I was the laughingstock of the sixth grade. To make matters worse, there were things they called "Report Cards." I remember opening my first report card and wondering why there were so many grades written in red. When I showed my report card to our boarding father, he was outraged. He sat me down in my room and rebuked me for not trying hard enough and for being lazy. After he left, I sat in my room alone and cried. I wondered what would ever become of me, since I could not get school right.

By the time I got to high school, my teachers and advisors were counseling me to forget about college and go to a trade school instead. Back in those days, that was the supreme insult: that one was not smart enough even to apply to college. When I returned to the United States for my senior year, I found that high school was much easier in America; I made almost all A's and was accepted by one of the three colleges I applied to. I eventually graduated from college and was even accepted into Princeton Theological Seminary. But when I sent out invitations for my ordination, one of my former boarding parents said she just had to come because if she did not see it with her own eyes, she would never believe that I was becoming ordained as a Presbyterian minister!

I share this to give God all the glory. God has a way of taking those whom society might disregard as failures or those who will never amount to much and using them. My life is a testimony to God's gracious love and power.

After that difficult first year in boarding school, my parents went on a one- year furlough. By this time, there were six of us children. My sister Louise was born in Mashhad the year I was in sixth grade in Tehran. Then Ruthie was born while we were living in Philadelphia. We were staying in the home of my grandfather, who had been a bachelor for many years since his wife had died in her fifties. I can only imagine the adjustment he had to make to having a family with six children living in his relatively small home. I attended Wagner Junior High School for my seventh-grade year in Oak Lane, a suburb of Philadelphia. It was a real culture shock after my last experience in Tehran. I did get a paper route and delivered the Philadelphia Evening Bulletin, which afforded me about three to four dollars of income a week. For the first time in my life, I was actually earning money. Most of that year is a blur, but I remember how hot it was on the third floor where Lennie and I had our room and that my mother would take us for walks to get us out of the house for some fresh, cool air.

My family returned to Iran, and I went back to boarding school for grades 8 through 11. This time, my father was assigned to the Christian hospital in Hamadan. We moved into a big house on the hospital grounds. The summers in Hamadan were delightful since the mission had a property called Nurmahal ("place of light"), which was a few miles outside the city limits. It was a very old building with designated screened-in sleeping areas on the second floor. There was nothing quite like falling asleep with the gentle summer breezes blowing over you. As a boy, I loved it when we would spend a few days there. There was also a tennis court and a swimming pool.

One summer we lived in Hamadan, the Iranian youth group invited me to go hiking with them up Alvand mountain, which lies on the outskirts of Hamadan. It was 11,759 high — a challenging hike. The plan was that we would meet before dawn and get to the peak before the afternoon storms rolled in. I came prepared with a canteen of safe drinking water and some sandwiches. As we began our ascent in the foothills, only one person had thought to bring a flashlight, so we all held hands and followed the person with the light. On the way, we passed nomads grazing their flocks and selling some of their goats' milk products. We made it to the top and sat there eating our lunches. By then, I had drunk all my water and was very thirsty. My mother had forbidden me to drink any of the refreshing clear water that flowed in the many brooks we passed because of the potential danger of bacteria or parasites. My Iranian friends all enjoyed the water, but I abstained. When I arrived home and sat down at our dining room table, I drank sixteen classes of water. When I read the words of the Psalmist, "As a deer pants for flowing streams, so my soul pants for you, O God. My soul thirsts for God, for the living God" (Psalm 42:1-2), I am reminded how thirsty I was that day I climbed Alvand and hope that I might continue to have the same thirst for God.

Hamadan was a historic city. Queen Esther's tomb was not too far from our home. When we had guests from other cities, they all wanted to visit her grave. A Jewish synagogue marked her grave, and I can still see the big scrolls containing the Torah that dominated the small room. I had a very special feeling standing there thinking of how brave Esther had been and how her life had influenced many generations.

The primary way I navigated the town was by bike. The hospital was at the end of BooAli street which ran through town to the main square. It was always fun going into town since it was all downhill, but it was very challenging to pedal my bike up the steep incline to get to my house. One day I had gone to the main square and was stopped at the light when a big policeman came up to me and grabbed the handlebars of my bike. In a very authoritative voice, he barked a question that I had never heard before: "Have you completed your military service?"

I thought to myself, *What is he talking about? I am an American citizen and who does he think he is stopping me and challenging me this way?* I looked right at him and said, "I am an American and I do not have to do any military service!" Surely my confident answer would settle the issue and I could be on my way. But no! Mr. Policeman was not swayed by my youthful swagger. He repeated his question. This time, he firmly gripped the handlebars of my bike; I felt a wave of fear sweep over me. I remembered seeing army trucks driving through a village and soldiers nabbing young boys and forcefully taking them off to military service. I explained that my father was the director of the American Hospital and that I was not Iranian. This seemed to anger him all the more, and he rebuked me for lying to him. "Do you think I am a fool? You sound like an Iranian to me!" I became desperate. I slipped my hand into my pocket and ran my fingers over a ten-toman bill I had planned to use for buying some ice cream. The thought came that I was going to have to give it up or be arrested and taken to military service. That thought prompted me to take the ten tomans out of my pocket and offer Mr. Policeman a gift, which immediately did the trick. He took the money and let go of my handlebars. I was a free man again. I am not proud of what I did, but I saw no other alternative. At sixteen, I was beginning to see the gray areas of the culture in which I lived.

Back to Tabriz

Once again, my father was asked to relocate, but this time it was to Tabriz and I was overjoyed. I was grateful that I had had the opportunity to live in Mashhad, Hamadan, and Tehran, but Tabriz had always held a special place in my heart. I spent the following school years in Tehran and the summers in Tabriz. As a guest resident in Iran, I did not have permission to be formally employed, so when any kind of side job opportunity presented itself, I was always excited that I might be able to make some money.

One summer, an American construction company from North Carolina was building barracks for NATO and the engineers were looking for a translator. Someone suggested they hire me, and I jumped at the opportunity to earn some money. I lived in the barracks with the American engineers and followed them around in their pickups and translated for them. After a few weeks of sitting around a lot, I got drawn into helping mix concrete. I made $400 that summer and I thought I was a rich man.

Another summer during my high school years, my father asked me to serve as the registrar of the hospital. I was not particularly excited about this summer job, but it was all that I could find and it was only half day, so I could spend the afternoons swimming and playing tennis. I would sit in a little room with a small window and the patients first drew a number, which they got on a first-come-first-serve basis. Then they stood in line to see me. Many of our patients in those days were uneducated and thus they could not fill out the forms. All the records were written in English, so my job was to help them fill out the forms they needed. The biggest challenge for me was all the different ways to spell

Stewart Family in Tabriz

Iranian names. I soon discovered that there were many creative ways to spell names, so I did my best to sound them out and fill in the registration cards. Many patients did not even know how old they were, so I had to guess. One particular village lady stands out in my mind. I asked her if she was married. "Oh yes," she declared proudly. Then I asked what her husband's name was. She again responded with enthusiasm, "His name is 'Agha,'" which is like saying her husband's name is "Mister." I replied, "I am sure he is a wonderful Agha, but does he have a name?" This time I was the one who was surprised. She replied, "All our marriage I have just called him Agha, and that is all I know about his name." This dear village girl had married a man whose name she did not even know, and it had never occurred to her to find out. As I looked out into the waiting room full of patients, I saw the hospital chaplain sitting with people and sharing the love of Christ. His name was Reverend Azzizi. He was an Assyrian pastor from Rezaieyh. He was humble and kind and spent hours with hurting, broken people. Each day, he visited the patients in their rooms and hung up a Bible story picture, then told the story to the patients. The remainder of the day, they could look at the picture and think about the story they had heard earlier. Only heaven knows how many sick, hurting people in our hospital are in glory because of the love and devotion of this man! I became very good friends with his two boys. Many years later, I visited Rev. and Mrs. Azzizi in Chicago. They were in their nineties, but what a joyful welcome I received! Since they did not know English or Persian very well, we communicated in Azeri Turkish. It made me feel like I was a young boy back in Tabriz again.

    The hospital was unable to pay me for my services after all, but I am grateful for the heartwarming experiences I had that summer meeting everyday people from a number of backgrounds. Was God preparing me for things to come?

    As summers go, the most interesting summer I had during my high school years was the summer I received an invitation from Cuyler Young Jr. who was a prominent archaeologist associated with the University of Pennsylvania. He and his team, which included his wife, were excavating a distinguished dig in northwestern Iran at a site call "Hassanloo," which was named for the village that was next to it. Another American boy, who was a friend and classmate of mine, and I were given the honor of spending a summer in this small Iranian village. Our living arrangements were very simple. The local schoolhouse became our lodging place. It was a one-story building with several rooms, a kitchen, and an outhouse. My friend and I slept on the flat mud roof, which meant we were awakened very early in the morning by the sunrise. But the evenings were cool, and it did not rain all summer, so it was a real treat to lie on wooden beds and gaze at the hosts of stars that formed a heavenly canopy over us. At noon each day, the Iranian cook who had been hired to cook for the team served us a delicious Persian dish. We spent the evenings listening to the archaeologists speculate about what life must have been like thousands of years ago. That summer, I fell in love with the ancient history of Iran.

To avoid the midday heat, we started to work early in the morning. My job was to follow the archeologists and interpret for them. All the workers were Azeri Turks, so I had the job of communicating where they should dig and, in some cases, how they should dig. I must confess that I enjoyed the authority that had been given to me. As the summer dragged on, I learned more and more about how to respect a dig and was even given small assignments. I remember uncovering a skeleton with great care and was very delighted to hear that I had done a very professional job. We worked until about two in the afternoon and then took a break until about four and then worked for a few more hours.

This experience left such an impression on me that during my junior year in high school at Community School, I decided to conduct my own dig and write a term paper on what I discovered. I knew that Ray, a city that lies south of Tehran, was an ancient city and that there was an old mound there that might hold some archeological secrets. So, I ventured down to Ray and spent several hours digging and gathering potshards. Later in college, I chose to major in history and wrote my senior thesis on Afghanistan's foreign policy post-World War II. My time in Iran had created in me a longing to study political science hoping to become an American diplomat to Iran. I thought to myself, *So many of the diplomats that I met did not know the language and only stayed in Iran a few years.* I proudly thought I could do a much better job.

I cannot leave the wonderful summer in Hassanloo behind quite yet without sharing one other experience. I had become good friends with the "katkhoda," which literally means the god of the village. He was a friendly man in his mid-forties. He had a big, bushy mustache and a radiant smile. One day he asked if he could speak to me; his face conveyed he had something very serious to tell me. He pulled me behind the dump truck and in almost a whisper he said, "I want you to marry my daughter." In Turkish, it would sound this way: "I want you to *buy* my daughter."[6] Now I was only sixteen, and I later learned his daughter was twelve. His words kindled a fear in me that I never remembered having before. I wanted to be as respectful as I could, but I had to make it clear that I was not in the mood for getting married to a twelve-year-old girl from Hassanloo whom I had never seen. He must have clearly seen how I recoiled in disbelief, for he quickly departed, saying, "Well, you think about it." The rest of the summer, I had to find ways to avoid him every time he came around so as not to disrespect him.

---

6. The word "almak" means both "to buy" and "to marry" — showing the importance of learning a language within its cultural context.

He must have thought to himself, *Here is an American who speaks Azeri Turkish and if I get him to marry my daughter, who knows how many doors that would open for me?* The end of the summer brought special relief as I headed back to Tabriz and to the safety of my home in the big house in the hospital compound.

CHAPTER FIVE
MY IDENTITY

My spiritual journey began at age six. My family was living in Philadelphia after a five-year term in Tabriz, and my father was engaged in furthering his medical studies now that he had spent four years practicing medicine in Iran. I was in the first grade and was taller than my first-grade teacher, Mary George. She was of Armenian descent and lived with her sisters. Our families remained friends for years. One day, while attending Sunday school, Miss George said something that greatly disturbed me. "Everyone is either going to heaven or hell." I realized I had no idea *where* I was going! Arriving at home that day, I knew this issue had to be resolved immediately. I found my mother in the kitchen and in all seriousness asked, "Mom, am I going to heaven or hell?" Her answer was even more troubling: "I'm not sure, Tat." Now, when your own mother does not know whether you are going to

Tat, age 6, with his family

heaven or hell makes the issue even more devastating. But she did not leave it there. "Let's make sure today that you are going to heaven." She went over the gospel and I affirmed I was a sinner and in need of the saving grace of Jesus. She had me pray the sinner's prayer, and I finally found peace.

My mother was a wonderful Bible teacher and spent many hours teaching us children. I never doubted the Bible until I went to Community School in Tehran and was confronted by teachers who did not have the same faith and trust in it. I made new friends who were not believers, and the world began to press in on me. Having been a poor student at home was not the problem, but being a poor student in an actual school drove me to look for meaning elsewhere; for me, it was on the basketball court. Thankfully, my friends did not use drugs or drink alcohol. They did smoke, and I tried that for a while; but since I wanted to be an outstanding athlete, I quickly gave it up.

My high school years contained both agony and ecstasy. The agony was in going to class. Not being able to read was a huge handicap; but even worse than that, it was a source of deep embarrassment and shame. I now realize how deeply it scarred me to be one of the worst students in my class. In Farsi, we say I was the "class' garbage." Is there any wonder I hated school?

Once the last bell rang and I was released from school for the day, I ran to the basketball court. I was a lanky six-feet-four inches and towered over many of my classmates. Iranians are not known for being tall, and although there were other American kids in my school, most of my classmates were from the Middle East. I was the tallest basketball player on our school team. I spent as much time as I could on the court playing pickup games with whomever was available. It became my life and where I could salvage my reputation. Basketball made me popular and gave me a purpose for living. It became my idol. It took the place of God in my life. I loved it more than anything else. I trusted it to do for me what in reality God should have been doing. I served it with my time and my energy, when I should have been serving God first. God is a jealous God and He will see to it that our idols will fail us. He had to destroy my idol so that I would humbly submit my life to Him.

I can now see how God had his hand on me, most likely because of the faithful prayers of my mother. Twice during my high school years in Tehran, I experienced the most excruciating pain I had ever had in my life. While breathing hard playing basketball, I felt as though someone had stabbed me in the chest with a knife. Both times I was taken to the American Army Hospital in Tehran. The diagnosis both times was that forty percent of my right lung had collapsed. Breathing was painful, to say the least. The first time, I was hospitalized for two weeks. The second time, a needle was inserted into my chest which drew out the fluid that had gathered on the top of my lung. Doctors thought a likely cause for my collapsed lung was all the concrete dust I had inhaled during my brief career mixing concrete for the

American construction company. In time, I recovered and life returned to normal.

My senior year, I attended South Hunterdon Regional High School in Lambertville, New Jersey, and had an exceptional year playing basketball as a starter on the varsity team. I received the Most Valuable Player award that year and brought home a trophy that I proudly displayed in my room. The next fall, my parents returned to Tabriz, as I began my freshman year at Davis and Elkins College in Elkins, West Virginia. As I was moving into my dorm room, I was carrying an armful of things — including my beloved trophy; as I opened the door to my dorm, it sprang back, hitting my arm and knocking my trophy out of my hands. I watched in slow motion as my trophy hit the ground and shattered into a thousand pieces! The symbol of my self-worth and success was gone. I stood there in disbelief! How could this have happened? I became depressed. The symbol of what I loved the most was now gone.

My first year at Davis and Elkins College was a very lonely time for me as I struggled to make new friends and deal with the overwhelming anxiety I felt in trying to understand college-level courses. I could not wait for basketball season to begin, so I could try out for the freshman team. I spent all my free time in the gym playing basketball. Thanksgiving weekend was particularly lonely, as most of my fellow students had gone home for the weekend. Having nowhere to go for the holiday, I passed the time in the college gym. I found a few students on the court playing a pickup game and I soon joined them. In the heat of the game, I jumped up to grab a rebound. As I snatched the ball, I felt a too familiar stab in my chest. I fell to the floor and lay there in agony. Fellow students offered to call for help, but I resisted, insisting that I would be fine. When I could finally manage my breathing by taking shallow breaths, I walked back to my dorm room and lay down on my bed. Fear swept over me as I recalled the two previous times I had endured this same pain. I was not sure what to do next. My roommate finally convinced me to call 911, and I waited for the longest time before the EMTs arrived. As I was wheeled out of my dorm, I was told that the one ambulance in Elkins was on another call, so they had sent a hearse to transport me to the Emergency Room at the local hospital. Riding to the hospital in a hearse did not instill a lot of hope, as I struggled for each breath!

When I finally saw a doctor, I told him what I thought my problem was. I told him this had happened before, and I was certain it was a spontaneous pneumothorax. I thought it would impress him I even knew the medical term. On the contrary, he scolded me and said that was impossible since there were no external puncture wounds. He then ordered an X-ray to prove me wrong. An hour later, he returned and sheepishly admitted that my diagnosis was correct. I was admitted to a ward of a dozen male patients. Most of them had black lung from working in the coalmines.

Many of them chewed tobacco, and all night long I heard them spitting into their spittoons. I was eventually put in a private room, but the doctors had no plan for my healing other than bed rest. It was a dark and lonely time.

My relationship with God was already at a very low ebb. I had tried going to church on Sundays, and the only church within walking distance was the local Presbyterian congregation. The usher who distributed the church bulletins had cheerfully welcomed me, but no one ever spoke to me and no one ever invited me to their home for a meal. Even though the church was very close to my college, they had no special programs for college students, nor did they have a ministry to them. It did not take long for me to give up on going to church; and now the God who I thought loved me had ruined my life again. So, I lay in my hospital bed and stewed in my anger at God! I found myself continually punching the wall with my fist for hours on end. I never reached out to God. I was too angry!

In early December, a wonderful family from Philadelphia who had been friends of my parents drove all the way to Elkins, West Virginia, to rescue me. They took me into their home and helped me contact my parents in Iran. My father, accompanied by my little sister Ruthie, arrived soon after in America. My father arranged for me to see a specialist who confirmed that I had a collapsed lung. During my consultation with him, the specialist gave me a choice: I could have surgery to take care of the problem once and for all, or I could choose not to do any more aggressive physical activity. In other words, *no more basketball.* I could not imagine life without the ability to exercise, let alone playing my beloved sport of basketball. They performed the surgery in January 1966. My father prayed over me as they wheeled me into the operating room. The next thing I remembered was seeing my father sitting at the end of my bed in the recovery room. It was so comforting knowing he was there.

The surgeon later explained to me that he had grafted my right lung to my ribcage so that it could not collapse again. I now had a 14-inch scar that went halfway around my side. The most difficult part was dealing with the challenges of rehab. I developed pneumonia, so was started on high doses of penicillin every four hours. The injections were extremely painful and soon I had no more places on my body that did not hurt. There were two people I hated to see: the nurse who had to give me the next injection, and the physical therapist who was trying to get me to move my arm. Yet despite all that I was going through, I did not reach out to God for help. I was too proud.

Then one day in January during a very severe snowstorm, the Rev Glen Knecht, who had been a missionary in Tabriz and whom I had not seen since my last days in Iran, appeared at the door of my hospital room. Despite the very heavy snowstorm that had closed many roads, he had found his way to the Presbyterian Hospital in Philadelphia. He was serving as the senior pastor of the Oxford Presbyterian church in Pennsylvania. He greeted me with his customary warm smile. After inquiring how I was doing, he asked a very penetrating question: "Tat, how is your relationship with the Lord?" Not the question I really wanted to hear. With little hesitation, but dripping with hypocrisy, I replied, "I am doing just fine with the Lord." He then read a Psalm and prayed with me. And just as suddenly as he had appeared, he was gone. What happened next changed my life forever.

As I lay in my bed, I felt the presence of the Holy Spirit in a way I had never before experienced. It felt like a great pressure on my chest. The best way I can describe it is to say it felt like a fifty-pound bag of flour had been placed on my chest, that God had pinned me to the bed and was asking me, "Will you now call upon Me for help? Will you now surrender your life to Me?" For the first time in months, I broke down and cried out to God, saying, "God, I am a sick and broken person. I have failed You at everything I have tried to do. But today, I give myself to You and You can do whatever You want to do with me."

The battle was over! I had surrendered!

For the first time in my life, a peace filled my heart and a hope in the Lord settled in, transforming my once hard and rebellious heart.

My father wanted me to go back to college before he returned to Iran, so we needed to find one near my doctor in Philadelphia. We reached out to Rev. Knecht again, who introduced us to the president of Lincoln University in Chester County. Because of the record snowfall, Lincoln was a week late starting the winter semester, so I had to be accepted as a special student.

Lincoln University was an African American school. It had been founded by Presbyterians during the "Separate but Equal" days after the Civil War, and included a seminary for preparing men for ordination. I found a warm reception as I moved into the freshman dorm. Once again, God set me in a special place for His purposes. His ways are not our ways. I would go on to graduate from Lincoln University in 1969.

What is it like to be a minority? In some ways, I have always been a minority. Having grown up in Iran, I stood out as a minority. Now at Lincoln, I was a very visible minority. What lesson was God trying to teach me? What I slowly learned was that my relationship with others had much to do with my own attitudes. I had to let God break any stereotypes I might have had, and relate to each person in love and acceptance, realizing that they may have had stereotypes about me. I had to learn to find my true self-worth in my relationship with God. Instead of retreating into my own white world, I tried to be an active member of my campus. I sang in the choir, joined the basketball team, and even pledged a fraternity for a few weeks. Soon, I discovered some true followers of Jesus in my dorm who invited me to join them in their rooms for Bible study and prayer. I experienced the power of the gospel in breaking down prejudice, a lesson that has lived in my heart ever since.

The first few weeks at Lincoln were not easy. My father had returned to Iran, and I did not know anyone. One Saturday morning at about ten in the morning. someone knocked on the door of my dorm room. I was still in bed, but threw on some clothes and answered the door. There stood Rev. Knecht with his beaming smile. I invited him in and we sat and talked for a while. He then gave me a set of car keys to his second car along with a gas credit card and said, "You will be lonely at times and I want you to have the means to come to church and visit our home any time you want." Thus began a very wonderful relationship with Glenn and Betty Knecht and their family. Most Saturdays, I went to their home and did my laundry, and on Sundays, I attended the Oxford Presbyterian Church. I even babysat for them and did odd jobs around the house. They became my family away from home. I can't express enough my gratitude to Glenn and Betty Knecht for the role they played in my spiritual growth and in modeling a Christ-centered marriage and home. It was also through their influence that I began to help with the church youth group, and it was through his preaching that I eventually heard the call to ministry during my junior year in college.

Another amazing event which would shape my future occurred my first day of World History Class. I had just taken a cursory glance at the name of my instructor: "Dr. Andrew Murray." As I slipped into a seat in the last row, I was astonished at the appearance of Dr. Murray. He looked just like Patty's father, whom I had known in Iran. I knew that he certainly wasn't Patty's father, but he could have been his twin! Then, in one of his lectures, he mentioned he had a brother who had been a missionary to Iran. Now the mystery was solved. It brought back many fond memories of Patty from our time together in boarding in Tehran, and I thought it really would be nice to know how she was doing. So, I got up enough courage to ask Dr. Murray if he could give me Patty's address. Thus began a new chapter of my life as I reached out to Patty and we began corresponding.

In the fall of 1966, it suddenly occurred to me I had no place to go for Christmas break. So, I wrote Patty a sob story about how I would have to spend Christmas break all by myself in the dorm. From what I am told, when Patty shared my shameless appeal to her merciful heart, her mother's response was, "Oh, let's invite the big galoot here!" And so, I went to Denver for Christmas and was reunited with Patty and her family. It was one of the most fun Christmases I had ever had just being with the Murrays. But the most important part of the story is that I fell in love with Patty. The following summer, we both took jobs in Estes Park, Colorado, and grew much closer. That summer on a moonlit night on the edge of Mary's Lake, I asked Patty to marry me. Our courtship was mostly long distance since I had to return to Pennsylvania. We wrote many letters, but the one that probably was the most shocking for Patty was when I informed her I felt called to the ministry and would go to seminary. As she tells it, "That means that I will have to become a minister's wife!" We were married in Denver in 1969. I went off to Princeton Seminary and Patty continued her nursing studies at Southern Colorado State College (its name at the time) in Pueblo. Needless to say, that was a very hard year for both of us. I have never been so happy to see the end of a school year!

Later I would learn how my father-in-law had become a missionary to Iran. Dr. Thomas Murray was born in Portland, Pennsylvania to Rev. and Mrs. Thomas Murray. Rev. Murray was serving in a Presbyterian church in Pennsylvania when his son was born. In the early months of my father-in-law's life, a missionary from Iran named Rev. Frederick G. Coan was a guest preacher. My father-in-law's father, Rev. Murray, asked if he would be willing to baptize his newborn son? Rev. Coan agreed. After baptizing him, he consecrated him to serving God in Iran. Years later, after my father-in-law finished medical School and was serving as a captain in the Army in Panama, he and his bride-to-be Nancy Lounsbery applied to the board of foreign Missions to serve in China. But the Board rejected that application and suggested Iran. Soon after being married, they boarded a ship which had served as a troop carrier, The Marine Carp, during World War II and sailed for Beirut, Lebanon, then on to Iran. Their first post of service was Mashhad, where Patty was born, July 30, 1948.

Tat and Patty's Engagement Photo, 1968

When Patty's grandfather was a student in Princeton Theological Seminary, he was a classmate of Rev William McElwee Miller. Dr. Miller had had been deeply touched by the life and ministry of Dr. Samuel Zwemer who had visited Princeton and challenged students to heed the call to evangelize the Muslim world. When Thomas Murray Sr. was urged by Dr. Miller to go to Iran, he protested, saying he had not felt called by the Holy Spirit. Interestingly enough, when Patty's father and mother did arrive in Iran, Dr. Miller happened to be quite ill and it was suggested that the newly arrived Dr.

Murray pay him a medical visit. When Rev. Miller heard that Dr. Thomas Murray was coming to see him, he initially thought that it was his old classmate from Princeton. How delighted he was, however, to hear that it was the son of the man he had tried to recruit for Iran years before.

My parents arrived a year later to begin their term of service in Tabriz (1947), and I first met my future in-laws the following year when there was a first-termers conference in Tehran. There were, I believe, over fifty Presbyterian missionaries in Iran at that time. Patty's mother asked my mother if she wanted to see her newborn baby girl. So, as we have often been reminded, my mother, with me in her arms, paid a visit to my future bride. God brought our lives together when I was two years old and Patty was two weeks old — and as I write this, we have

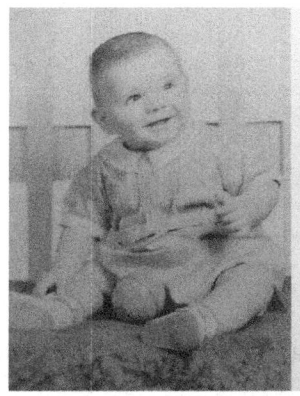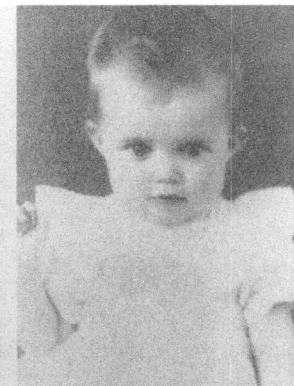

Tat and Patty, Baby Pictures

been married for over fifty years (neither of us recalls that first introduction).

Our fathers had each been dedicated at birth to serve in the Muslim world and our parents were colleagues who served side by side in Iran.

I attended Community School with Patty and we both lived in the same boarding facility.

We knew each other in high school but then lost contact as the Murrays returned to Denver, while the Stewarts returned to Philadelphia.

Then, because of my collapsed lung and subsequent surgery, I had to drop out of Davis and Elkins, College in West Virginia, winding up at Lincoln University where one of my first classes was World History with Dr. Andrew Murray, which led me to be reconnected to Patty Murray.

There is no doubt in my mind that God brought us together from common backgrounds to prepare us for a life neither of us had ever imagined! God brought us together and has woven our lives into an amazing tapestry that He is still working on to this day.

CHAPTER SIX
SEMINARY

After living in the men's dorm at Princeton Seminary my first year, it was a great joy to move into the married students' housing with Patty. We had very little money, so Patty asked me what our budget was for furnishing our apartment. I had not really thought about it; but, feeling very generous, I announced we could spend $50! We visited a junk furniture store in Trenton, NJ and were able to buy a few furnishings.[7] We slept on the floor for a few days until the bed we ordered arrived. Despite not having many of the comforts of life, we were filled with hope that I was now on my way towards completing my seminary studies and closer to my calling to becoming an ordained Presbyterian minister. Patty soon found a job as a nurse in an extended care facility and we settled into campus life.

Tat and Patty Wedding Photo, 1969

After two years of the academic world, I longed for more hands-on ministry. When Patty's home church

---

7. "Furnishings" included: one drop-leaf dining table which regularly "dropped" our meals onto our laps, four chairs held together with wire, and one lumpy green easy chair. I built our sofa using a large pine box, a mattress, and some Persian fabric.

invited me to be an intern pastor for 15 months, both Patty and I jumped at the opportunity to go back to Denver and be closer to her family. We rented a small apartment in a rundown old house next door to First Avenue Presbyterian Church in Denver. Patty found a nursing job in downtown Denver, working in a doctor's office. Our main ministry accomplishment was to encourage the elders to support a coffee house ministry to reach the many runaway kids who flocked to Denver. I wanted to rent a storefront, but I had to have the permission of the elders of the church and ask if they would help with the rent. I was full of faith that this ministry was what God wanted us to do, so I asked them to pay the first month's rent and that we would trust God for the subsequent funds for future rent. Normally, elders do not agree to such proposals, but these elders agreed. For all the months that we rented that storefront, "The SONshine Inn," God was faithful to provide the funds we needed to pay the rent.

In 1971-1972, the "Jesus Movement" was sweeping across the country. At the same time, many kids from the Midwest were running away from home to the big city. Patty and I spent hours with these runaway kids, sharing the gospel with them. One of those young drifters was a man named John Wilson. I first met him on South Broadway Street; he was barefoot and wore shabby clothes. He told me he was hungry, so I took him out to dinner and bought him a sandwich. We talked for many hours that day, as he explained he was an actor who had come to Denver looking for work but had been unsuccessful. I asked him to come see me the next day at church, but I had little hope of ever seeing him again. Amazingly, he showed up. He said, "What did you do to me yesterday?" "What do you mean?" I asked. "Well, I gave my life to Jesus last night and threw up all night long. It was as if God was cleaning me from the inside out." There was no doubt about it: God had redeemed John from the streets of Denver to go to seminary and become a pastor. Years later, I was at a Billy Graham crusade in the

Tat and Patty with VW van, 1972

Washington DC area serving as a counselor, when a well-dressed man in a blue suit approached me and asked if I was Tat Stewart. I nodded, and he inquired, "Do you remember me? I'm John Wilson!" He was now the Director of Evangelism for his denomination. God had taken John from the streets of Denver, where he had surrendered his life to Christ and was using him to touch multitudes for Christ.

Patty and I had many amazing experiences that year and a half that we lived in Denver. Patty played her guitar and led worship, followed by testimonies and sharing the Good News of Christ.

It was not easy to pack our belongings and return to Princeton for my final year. By this time, we had hoped to start a family. Three years had gone by and Patty still had not gotten pregnant. Back in Princeton, we decided it was time to find out why, so we made an appointment with a doctor. The doctor ordered some tests and informed us that most likely we would not be able to have children. This news came as quite a blow to both of us. I remember sitting in our car in the parking lot, stunned by the news and not sure what to do next. I had just read a book on the power of praising God in all things, and, wanting to be very pastoral, I gently suggested we praise God for this news. Apparently, my words brought little comfort to Patty as we wept together. As the months passed, we were resolved to the fact that, for some unknown reason to us, God did not want us to have children. Then one morning Patty complained of being nauseated, and she found it hard to get out of bed. After a few days of feeling bad, I took her to the University clinic, and the doctor ordered a pregnancy test. The doctor soon returned and said, "This may not be good news, but you are pregnant." Patty yelled, "Praise the Lord!" The doctor was taken by surprise because most women at the university did not *want* to get pregnant! But we went home rejoicing what God had done that man had declared impossible.

Patty and I had been reading I Thessalonians together, and the passage that evening deeply touched us: "And we sent Timothy, our brother and minister of God, and our fellow laborer in the Gospel of Christ, to establish you and encourage you concerning your faith," (I Thessalonians 3:2) (NKJ) Patty immediately said, "It's going to be a boy, and we'll name him Timothy!" Being a major in pastoral care, I gently reminded her that there was a fifty-fifty chance of our baby being a girl. But Patty was adamant that it would be a boy. And, of course, she turned out to be right. We named our son Timothy, born July, 1973.

There were two more milestones in my faith during my last year in seminary. When Patty became pregnant, we felt it best for her to stop working, so I painted houses several days a week with a fellow seminarian who had a painting company. In those last months of seminary, we struggled financially, but we also saw God's wondrous provision. Our weekly grocery budget was only $15, and we had to watch every cent to make ends meet.

During one of those times when we just could not see how we were going to make it financially, we prayed, asking God for help. A few days later, an envelope was slipped under the door to our apartment. I quickly picked it up and opened it and was shocked to find a hundred-dollar bill with no accompanying note of explanation. To this day, I do not know where that money came from, but it was a wonderful reminder of how God provided for our needs.

Tat and Dr. Miller at Tat's Graduation

As time drew closer to my graduation from Seminary, my stress grew more intense as Patty was pregnant and due in July, and I had no job offers. Both Patty and I wanted very much to find a church in Colorado. Her parents lived there, and I loved the high elevation and dry climate. The *one* place I did not want to live in was New Jersey and I had often expressed my feelings to God and told Him I was ready to serve Him any place but New Jersey. One day, when I was meeting with the pastor of the church I was serving on weekends, I complained about how God had not provided a call for me in Colorado and time was running out. He looked me straight in the eye and said, "Tat, why are you limiting God?" I was stunned by the question. What, me limiting God? He said, "Why not tell God you will go wherever He calls you?" I knew he was right and shared his counsel with Patty; that evening we tearfully surrendered our future to wherever God would call us. The very next Monday, as I was walking out of the Seminary library, a classmate walked up to me and said, "Why didn't I think of you?" I looked at him, puzzled. "My uncle is the chairman of the search committee of his church and he has been asking me for names of the graduating class. Can I give him your name?" I was desperate for a job and I said, "Sure! Where is this church?" "Carteret." Of course. A few weeks later, I was called to be the pastor of the First Presbyterian Church of Carteret — *New Jersey*. Another lesson learned: never tell God where you will not go or what you will not do.

Graduation day arrived, and I marched down the aisle of the chapel at Princeton University. It was a day filled with much pomp and ceremony. After the service, Patty and I were standing in the courtyard greeting friends when an old friend, who himself was a graduate of Princeton Seminary, came over to congratulate me on my graduation: Dr. William M. Miller. After exchanging pleasantries, he informed us he wanted to have a special prayer of dedication for us. Patty was almost nine months pregnant and was eager to go home. But Dr. Miller was persistent. He pulled us aside and laid his fatherly hands on me and prayed a passionate prayer for us, which ended in his dedicating us to serve Christ in Iran. At that moment, I had no idea of how God would answer that prayer. All I knew was that I had to move my family to Carteret, find an obstetrician to deliver our baby, and begin pastoring a new congregation.

Dr. Miller Praying for Tat and Patty at Tat's Graduation

Soon afterwards, we moved into the manse of the Carteret church. It was the first time in our young marriage that we had a house to call home. Our neighbors were wonderful and soon we made new friends who would become lifelong friends. Our son Timothy was born in July and we began to learn how to be parents. My ministry soon became defined by reaching out to the youth of Carteret, and we saw many come to Christ and a number go into ministry. I faced many new challenges as a novice pastor. During the first year alone, I became a father for the first time, officiated my first communion service, performed my first wedding, moderated my first elders' meetings, and faced a church which was experiencing serious financial issues and some very challenging pastoral care situations. For the first time in my life, I found myself a nervous wreck. I did not handle conflict well, and that drove me to depression. I was eager to be a success and yet was not seeing results. Every Sunday during the worship service, I asked for any visitors to raise their hands, but there never were any. My preaching did not seem to bring any changes to people's lives and I could feel the frustration in the congregation. During the week, I often went off alone into the sanctuary to pray. One particular morning, my frustration seemed to have reached a boiling point. As I prayed, I found myself saying, "God, I quit. I can't do this anymore. I want to return this church to You. I am through!" As I uttered these words out loud, I felt a burden lifted off my heart and I began to laugh. It was as though all the pent-up frustrations and anger in my heart were draining out of me. I kept laughing. I couldn't stop. Several minutes went by, followed by an amazing peace. I felt God was saying, "This church was never yours, it has always been Mine. You just need to trust Me and lean on Me and I will be at work." That day changed me as well as my approach to ministry. God revealed to me that my eyes had been on my ministry, and not on God. In a not-so-subtle way, I was worshiping my ministry instead of God. It was a life-changing lesson that prepared me for some of the challenges that I would face later on in my ministry.

Two years later, our daughter Emily was born. Patty had desperately wanted a girl, as did I. While Patty was pregnant, she went through some challenging times in her faith and at one point prayed that if God really loved her, He would give her a daughter. And He did! What we did not know then was that God was only going to give us two children. We had been told by doctors that we could not have children, but God proved the doctors wrong by giving us two. During those years that we thought we would remain childless, God was teaching us a very important lesson: He always advances His kingdom through trouble. It was difficult to realize we could not have children, but it also pressed us closer to God and we saw Him doing something amazing in our lives by giving us two of them! But not only was His kingdom advanced in our lives, our story gave hope and encouragement to others. Paul's words, "I want you to know brothers, what has happened to me has really served to advance the Gospel" (Phil. 1:12) came alive for me. It became a way of looking at life. When trouble comes, watch and wait to see how God will use it to advance His kingdom. Even if your prayers remain unanswered, God may be opening doors elsewhere for the spread of His kingdom.

After a few years as pastor of the Carteret Church, I became restless. I looked for new ministries within my current ministry. I threw myself into youth retreats and summer camping programs. But my heart was longing for something more. I wanted to make a difference in the world for Christ and often felt I was not doing much of anything worthwhile for God. But I remained faithful and obedient to my calling, praying for God to lead me and use me as He desired. In the spring of 1977, I was away for the weekend at a Junior High retreat. Patty phoned me, an unusual occurrence because of poor phone connections. There was an excitement in her voice as we talked. Then what she said next made me fear something terrible had happened. She said, "How would you like to serve as a pastor in Iran? We received a letter today from the Synod of the Evangelical Church in Iran inviting us to come to Abadan to pastor St. Christopher's Church." I was stunned. Was Patty actually ready to go to Iran? Every time I had entertained the thought about perhaps going back to Iran, I remembered my commitment to myself that I would never do that without Patty's full approval. I would not go back to Iran without Patty's feeling called, too. The letter came out of the blue and now Patty was saying that she believed this was from the Lord and that she was willing to go. She told me God had changed her heart instantly. After we hung up, I sat by the phone for a few minutes. It was one of those pivotal moments in one's life when one knows that this decision would change everything. I was lost in thought for most of the rest of the retreat, wondering what God had in store for us. Little did I know then that God would be moving us into a Revolution that would not only change Iran but would also change us forever.

CHAPTER SEVEN
GOING TO IRAN

The path from receiving the call to missions to actually arriving on the mission field is often much longer and arduous than one would imagine. There is a feeling that reminds me of a time I asked directions from a local man in the state of Maine, and he answered, "You can't get there from here!" I had known so many deeply committed Christians who felt called to the mission field but could never get there. Our story, at first, seemed to follow that same disappointing trail.

Our first hurdle was overcoming the fact that our congregation in Carteret thought we were insane for even considering returning to Iran. The news from Iran was very disturbing. The first tremors of the political earthquakes to come were being felt. On August 21, 1978, the Rex Movie theater in Abadan, Iran, burned to the ground with 377 people inside; many were injured and some perished as they were trampled to death by those trying to escape. The tensions were mounting as the government blamed terrorism. The daily news from Iran led to a mounting tension in our lives as well. We had informed our congregation of our call to serve as missionaries to Iran, and one Sunday, in the middle of my sermon, an elderly gentleman stood up and rebuked me in a loud voice, "Are you crazy?!?" Now in my entire, albeit short, career as a preacher, I had been called many things; but never "crazy." "You are going to get yourself and your family killed," he continued. By now, everyone had forgotten what I was preaching about and I was not so sure myself. I tried to calm him down by telling him our parents, who were both veteran missionaries from Iran, were very supportive of our going. I tried to reassure him we knew the culture and the language and that if God were calling us, He would also protect us. He finally calmed down, and we ended that service without further incident, but it added to our rising concerns about our future. We daily put our faith in Jesus that He would be faithful to complete that which He had begun in our lives.

In the days ahead, we completed all the mission's requirements, held a huge yard sale to get rid of our earthly belongings, and said goodbye to our loved ones. It was January 1979 when we drove down to Ventnor, New Jersey, to move into temporary housing until we could make the final arrangements for our departure to Iran. By now, the Revolution was in full sway in Iran, and on January 16, 1979, the Shah and his family departed Iran for the last time. This was a most inconvenient event for us, as it raised a very legitimate question: *Who is in charge of the Revolution?* That was a simple question for the multitudes in the streets of Iran who had brought about an unprecedented overthrow of the Pahlavi dynasty — Ayatollah Rouhollah Khomeini was the man of the hour. The New York Times reported a headline similar to: "Iran, Thursday, Feb. 1, 1979, Ayatollah Rouhollah Khomeini, the 78-year-old symbol of the Iranian revolution, returned in triumph to his homeland this morning and urged the expulsion of all foreigners from the country."

More than a thousand people, mostly men, packed into the airport to greet him. One banner waving in the hands of a loyal supporter read: "You are our religious, political, military, economic, and social leader!"

The New York Times again reported that the current government under the leadership of Prime Minister Shahpour Bakhtiar had issued a warning that if Khomeini tried to name anyone as provisional government leader, he would be arrested within hours.

The events of history are in the hands of God and we are left to seek His face and wait to see how He unfolds His will for each of us. For my family and me, our lives were on hold. I had severed my relationship with the Carteret Church and planned to move to Iran. But now the door was closed. Closed doors force one to wonder about how correctly one had discerned God's call in the first place. With these thoughts rattling around in my head, time in our missionary apartment passed slowly. Each day simply increased the frustration that we all felt. We were also in the midst of a severe blizzard with two small children who were easily bored. Needless to say, it was a very low point in our lives.

Then one day, we received some hopeful news. We learned that one of our contacts in Iran had approached the office of Ayatollah Mahmoud Taleghani, inquiring if the new government would permit foreigners to have a church and a pastor. At this point, there was not a clear central authority in Iran. There was the former government that the Shah had put in place, plus Ayatollah Khomeini, who had a formidable stronghold of power. In Shiite Islam, each Ayatollah has his own following based on his personality and theological interpretations of Islam. Ayatollah Taleghani was known for being an open-minded leader, and without hesitation, gave permission for the Community Church of Tehran to continue to meet for worship and to call a new pastor. It appeared God had turned the tide of history for us; Taleghani's office sent a telex to the Iranian Embassy in Washington, D.C. giving us permission to serve as pastor of the Community Church in Tehran. They informed us we were to appear in person at the Iranian Embassy on a certain day and time to receive our visas for Iran.

I will never forget the day we knocked on the door of the Iranian Embassy in Washington, D. C. It was a warm spring day and we were hot and weary from the long drive from Ventnor, New Jersey. The first thing that struck me was the stern and unfriendly faces of the people at the front desk. My experience in Iran had been that government officials had almost always greeted me with a respectful and friendly attitude. That friendliness was gone. Then I noticed that all the women wore head coverings (hejabs). I became nervous. We were finally called into another room where a clerk asked for our passports, which I respectfully gave him. It took only a few minutes for him to stamp the four-year, multiple entry, work permit visas into our passports. We thanked him and said goodbye and re-entered the world outside. It had felt as though we had been in Iran, yet it did not feel like the Iran we had known as children. It was a foretaste of what we would find when we eventually arrived in Tehran.

In July 1979, we boarded a British Airways 747 in New York bound for London. Days earlier, we had enjoyed a leisurely visit to London with my sister Peggie and her husband Andrew and their children. Then we checked in for our flight to Tehran. At this point, most major airlines were still flying to Tehran. Our flight first took us to Kuwait, where we remained on board until daybreak; we then departed for Tehran. As our plane touched down at its Mehrabad International Airport, we were not at all prepared for what we encountered. As we deplaned, we had to make our way through two lines of young men in green camouflage uniforms. My guess was that most of them were in their late teens. But what caught my immediate attention was that they were all carrying automatic rifles in their hands and looked at us with a most unfriendly gaze. We held our heads down and made our way into the terminal. As we waited for our bags to be unloaded, I noticed the terminal was full of men wearing yellow vests, and I soon discovered they were helping passengers with their luggage. As one of them passed by, I heard him speaking Azeri Turkish, so I greeted him in Turkish. He turned and smiled as he said, "Welcome home!" It felt so good to see his smiling face and to be welcomed back to Iran. But what he did next was unexpected. He shouted to the other baggage handlers and announced, "Our brother has come home." With that announcement, about a dozen men gathered around and all greeted us enthusiastically. What a wonderful feeling — it reminded me of the Iran we had left so many years before.

Not all of our encounters would be so pleasant.

We gathered our bags and breezed through customs. As we officially entered Iran, a delegation from the Evangelical Church of Iran greeted us, including Rev. Bob Pryor. It was heartwarming seeing a familiar face. Rev. Pryor had been my pastor in Tabriz when my brother Lennie and I had visited during our college years. They took us to the Sheraton Hotel for breakfast and a time to be reacquainted. It had been far too long since we had had fresh "barbari" bread with all the fixings and, of course, delicious Persian tea.

Rev. Robert Pryor had arranged for us to be hosted by an American family. The husband was the director of PanAm, and his wife had been the secretary of the Community Church, thus a good friend of Rev Pryor. They had a lovely home in Shemiran, a well-to-do suburb in northern Tehran. Wisely, Rev. Pryor let us begin our new life in Iran in a very American-friendly home to help us adjust to life in post-Revolution Iran. It was such a blessing not to have to endure drastic culture shock, as we could ease gradually into the Persian culture. It was very hot, so we stayed inside during the daytime close to the swamp cooler — "koolair" in Farsi. Later, we moved into Bob Pryor's home in North Tehran. We lived with him until we could find a place to rent.

Not long after our arrival, Patty and I, along with our son Tim and daughter Emily, were invited to attend a Synod meeting of the "Injili" (English) Evangelical Church to be officially welcomed. It had been years since we had spoken Farsi, and our Farsi was that of our youth, peppered with a lot of slang words. So, with our fractured Farsi, we did our best to follow what was going on. Then the moderator turned to us and asked if we had any prayer requests. Patty spoke right up: "Pray that God will lead us to a good place to rent." She had barely finished sharing our prayer request when the elder sitting next to her announced our prayers had already been answered. His name was Youash Benjamin; he was an elder in the Assyrian language Presbyterian Church. We arranged to see his apartment and found it very acceptable, especially since the Benjamin family had three daughters who could babysit our kids; one daughter attended Iran Zamin, an English language school, where our son Tim would attend first grade. This meant we could share in giving rides to our children. The year that followed, we had many good times with the Benjamin family and we are especially indebted to Mr. Benjamin, who assisted me in the many practical challenges of living in Tehran after the Revolution.

We soon realized that it was not advisable to go out after dark. We often heard gunshots. Because the police and military had been disbanded, each neighborhood organized a "Komeeteh" (Committee) to police their neighborhoods. Usually, these komeetehs were organized in the local mosque. So, we knew there were those who were watching over our neighborhood. Later, I learned roadblocks were in place as the komeetehs wanted to know who was coming and going. Also, most evenings our electricity went out, so we had many candlelit dinners. This meant our cooler would also go off, so we often sat in the darkness feeling the full blast of the summer heat. Then one night, everyone in the city was asked to ascend to their rooftops and in one accord shout, "Allah-o Akbar" (God is great!). What an eerily frightening sound this was! We lay on the living room floor, hoping not to be seen through the high glass windows. A city of a million people all on their roofs yelling "Allah is great" seemed to make the darkness of night seem even darker, with an intense sense of the presence of evil. How were we going to be able to share Christ with those who lived in this new Iran?

Tat, Patty, Tim, and Emily, 1979

There were other very practical challenges during those days, such as finding certain food items. Sometimes eggs were scarce, while other times it would be hard to find meat. But God provided for us in the most interesting ways. We had a little "Mom and Pop" corner store at the end of our block. I soon discovered that the owners were from Tabriz and, of course, spoke Turkish. It is not a secret in Iran that Turks take care of each other, so when they discovered I spoke Turkish, they became my guardians. When certain items were running low, they would always hold some back for me. When I entered their small shop, they asked if I needed eggs, and then some would appear from behind the counter. These men became our dear friends, and we often had wonderful conversations.

Another challenge was driving in Tehran. I had inherited a station wagon from the Community church which was a "Peykan" — much like the British Hillman but assembled in Iran. It was a good car for us, but it had one flaw. Because its design was British, it worked well in England's climate, but in Iran it was quick to overheat. Apparently, its radiator fan was not sufficient to keep it cool in the intense heat of Tehran. So, whenever I would get stuck in the very constant Tehran traffic, it would overheat, which led to my overheating as well! I had to turn off the engine at times and hope the traffic would not resume for a while; there was usually no worry about that.

The traffic in the inner city where we lived was intolerable. We could literally walk to our destinations more quickly than we could drive. I remember one day driving to St. Peter's church; I was stuck in traffic as usual and I saw a friend walking on the sidewalk and offered him a drive, thinking that at least we could have a friendly visit. He smiled graciously, but declined my offer, explaining, "Sorry, I am in a hurry." He was certain he could reach his destination faster on foot than by hitching a ride with me!

Also, the drivers in Iran had a new mentality that made driving difficult: they believed that now, in this new era of revolution, they were free from all traffic laws. If I stopped at a red light, drivers behind me would honk their horns and yell at me, "We are free now. We don't have to stop at red lights." I could not allow myself to go through a red light. I did notice, however, that the number of accidents at the major intersections were increasing daily. There seemed to be a good sermon illustration in this and years later, I found myself referring to what happens when we think we can live in direct disobedience to God's laws, which were given to us for our protection and blessing. Needless to say, I continued to stop at red lights, trying to ignore the blaring horns around me.

There was also the total absence of any police presence. It should surprise no one that when there are no police, people drive differently. But what I worried the most was what would happen if I, especially as an American, was involved in an accident? My Iranian friends coached me never to hit anyone in front of me, for that would be your fault. So, navigating motorbikes, three-wheel mini trucks, pedestrians and a sea of cars took total concentration. One day when I was driving down Ferdousi Avenue, the car in front of me suddenly stopped — I slammed on my brakes and the car behind me banged into me. I jumped out of my car to see the damage done and a nicely dressed gentleman disembarked from his car. When he saw me, he said in perfect English, "I think it is better that we do not attract a crowd. Here is my card, and let me know what it costs to fix your car." I immediately realized he was protecting me from what might have become mob law and the trouble that would have ensued. Seeing that the damage was minimal, I thanked him and resumed my journey. Once again, God had protected me.

The year we lived in Tehran, we observed continual demonstrations by masses of people. There was no way of knowing when the streets would swell with hundreds of people; and as an American, I knew they would not welcome me. After all, one of their main slogans was, "Death to America." As a result, I developed a sixth sense, which alerted me to potential danger. Often, I could drive around these demonstrations and find safer ways to navigate. But one day I got caught up in one with no easy escape. I was in my somewhat faithful Peykan, along with my two children, going north on Ferdousi Street, which was a one-way street. I saw that a block ahead there was an enormous crowd approaching carrying anti-American banners and shouting "Death to America!" Hemmed in on all sides by cars, I tried to maneuver to the right lane, hoping to find an alley to turn into. But no such opportunities were present. It soon became clear that I would have to follow the flow of the cars and blend into this demonstration. Both my children had blonde hair (Iranians have dark hair) so I threw a blanket over them in the back seat and told them not to move. My mind was assaulted by all kinds of unpleasant thoughts. What if this mob discovered we were Americans? What would they do to us? How would I ever be able to communicate to Patty what had happened to us? But the Holy Spirit, the Comforter, laid it on my heart to sing praises to God. As the hood of my car penetrated the crowd, and as hundreds of fists came pounding down on it, I sang louder. I sang in Turkish, in the hopes they would think I was an Iranian. The car swayed back and forth. My kids remained motionless and before I knew it, we had exited the mob on the other side. I quickly tried to assess any damage to the car, but thankfully there was none. But my heart was beating so fast I thought it might jump right out of my chest. I worshiped the Lord, who had once again saved me and my children. I have never forgotten that day and I am always reminded of Isaiah 43:2-3:

"When you pass through the waters, I will be with you: and through the rivers, they shall not overwhelm you. When you walk through the fire, you shall not be burned and the flame shall not consume you. For I am the Lord your God."

Since that day so long ago, I have often experienced the Lord's protection, but that day was one of the most dramatic and strengthened my faith not to fear but to overcome with the assurance of His presence and protection.

CHAPTER EIGHT
MINISTERING TO A CHURCH IN CRISIS

My official job description, by which my visa had been granted me, was pastor of the Community Church of Tehran. Rev. Bob Pryor had served for ten years as a Presbyterian missionary in Tabriz and Rasht. He was then called to be the senior pastor of the Community Church. He was one of the few western Christian workers who had weathered the actual Revolution. His mastery of the Persian language was exceptional and his commitment to serve the Christian community was obvious to all. When the Revolution was peaking, he sent his family back to the States while he remained. I once asked him how he had survived the dangers and chaos in the streets; he replied calmly, "I learned to sleep in the bathtub so I would not be hit by stray bullets."

Under Rev. Pryor's leadership, the Community Church had grown to over 600 members. It had been a thriving congregation before the Revolution. There were over 55,000 Americans living in Iran and many of them had lived in the capital city of Tehran. One evidence of the number of Americans living in Tehran was that there had been fourteen different English language congregations. In one way, it was discouraging that the American church had exported to Iran the idea that Christians could only worship in their own denominational churches. Community Church had begun years ago when Rev. John Elder, a Presbyterian missionary and a true Christian statesman, and others had decided they needed a church for expatriates who were living in Tehran; from its founding, it had been a church that embraced all who loved Jesus Christ.

It soon became apparent that I had been called to minister to a church in crisis. As the streets were burning and the turmoil continued to increase, most Americans were being evacuated. The U.S. government provided extra flights for the thousands of Americans who were ordered to leave. For many, the decision to leave Iran was made quickly; this meant that many American believers did not want to discard their possessions — especially their Christian books — so they brought them to the Church building in northern Tehran. I will never forget the day Rev. Pryor took Patty, the children, and me to see the church and we walked into many rooms that were filled waist high with books[8]. This is one way in which American Christians provided a blessing for the church in Iran. Patty and I organized the books into a wonderful theological library in my new Community Church office, which was in the basement of our apartment. After we left Iran, two wonderful Christian sisters moved into our apartment and found a great blessing in these books, and translated many into Farsi. Years later, these books were added to a historic library on the grounds of St. Peter's Evangelical church where many more Iranian believers could gain access to them.

St. Peter's Evangelical Church in Tehran

While we were exploring the church and surveying the situation, Rev. Pryor related to us what had happened when the Revolutionary guard had invaded the church. Apparently, they thought it was a "nest of spies"; when they saw the sound equipment, they were totally convinced. They held Rev. Pryor hostage in the church until they completed their investigation. At approximately 1 p.m., Rev. Pryor used the office phone to order "chelo kabab" (the national lunch of choice consisting of rice and barbecued meat) for everyone. He treated them like guests! Their entire demeanor changed. He had lived in Iran long enough to know that Iranians love guests and treat them with great respect. Rather than arguing with them or threatening them, he welcomed them and the incident ended peacefully.

---

8. There were also household items, toys, furniture, artwork, musical instruments, as well as a piano, a freezer, and some well-preserved mice!

Rev. Pryor later taught me what he had learned from his more than twenty years of experience in Iran about how to relate successfully to Iranian officials:

Be Polite. Do not raise your voice, always be respectful!

Be Patient. Do not show any agitation or anger, or any sense of being in a hurry.

Be Persistent. Do not take "no" for a final answer, but appeal to the person by sharing that you believe if there is anyone who can solve the problem, it is they.

As I was able to spend time with Rev. Pryor before he returned to the States to join his family, I realized again how important it has been for my growth as a minister of the gospel among the Iranian people to have had some very good mentors.

Another result of the quick departure of many Christians was that they left sizeable sums of money in their bank accounts. As Rev. Pryor was preparing me to become the pastor of the remnant, he took me to a bank and had my name added as a signature on the Community Church bank account. It shocked me to see there was over $50,000 dollars in that account. (That money would play a significant role later.)

In the summer of 1979, Community Church did not meet at all; but fall brought the return of many American teachers, so we made plans to reinstate worship services. However, this time we met at the German Lutheran Church in Northern Tehran on Friday mornings. The Lutherans worshiped on Sunday but because Friday was the official day off in Iran, we met on Fridays. In order to grow my flock, I contacted the Tehran Times, the only English language newspaper. They allowed me to run an ad for the Community Church for a reasonable price. The ad read: "Protestant English language worship on Friday at 10 a.m. Call the church for more information." I left it ambiguous so I could screen each call first and decide if I would give the caller our address. When we gathered for our first worship service in September of that year, there were six of us in worship; Patty began a Sunday school with only our two children as students. The church had diminished from 600 to 6. It was a bit discouraging, but we pressed on. Soon, a few teachers from Community School returned to Tehran and joined us. They helped me appoint a leadership council for the church, which was helpful. Others soon joined. A Nigerian family, a Japanese family, four young people from the Australian Embassy, a lady from Finland, an Irish lady and a few Iranian seekers who knew English began attending.[9] Potluck meals were quite the experience! I learned to eat a seaweed dish (sushi) provided by the Japanese family and a fried grasshopper casserole prepared by the Nigerian family. I wouldn't say I *liked* them, but for some reason, everyone expects the pastor to try all the dishes at church functions.

As the weeks passed, we became a close-knit fellowship. Everyone stayed for over an hour after church. We wanted to know how everyone was doing and what bits of news he or she might have about what was happening in our city. One of the new attendees was Mr. Bruce Laingen, the chargé d'affaire of the American Embassy. As a young man, his first assignment in Iran had been to Mashhad, where he had become good friends with Patty's family. He soon became a close friend. He always entered the church with a fully armed bodyguard who stood at the back of the sanctuary while I preached. In September, just weeks before the students overran the American Embassy and fifty-five Americans were taken hostage, Mr. Laingen invited Patty and me to the American Embassy for an evening of watching a movie together. We gladly accepted and spent an evening with a room full of U.S. government employees who, unbeknownst to any of us, would become hostages two months later. However, that night no one seemed to have a care in the world. I noticed everyone drank pretty heavily as we watched the movie "All the President's Men." Mr. Laingen was the only one of those in attendance that evening who had ever attended Community Church. As Patty and I drove away, the heavy metal gates of the American Embassy closed behind us, and we both felt uneasy as we reentered the streets of Tehran. We both agreed that it was not safe for us to return to the Embassy. We sensed the anti-American sentiment in the city and did not want our association with the Embassy to hurt our witness or to be a reason for the Iranian government to prevent us from remaining in Iran.

Our ministry to the dear people who attended Community Church was mainly to encourage them in their faith and offer a place of fellowship. One Friday, as I led worship, the gate to the church courtyard swung open and a tidal wave of men flooded the courtyard of the German Church. I hurried to see what was happening and was confronted by a middle-aged man with a skullcap who looked like he had not shaved for a month. In a loud and authoritative voice, he demanded to know what we were doing. He had a thick Turkish accent and so I replied in Turkish, with a boldness that could

---

9. Patty now taught Sunday School in English *and* Farsi — the Japanese and Nigerian kids knew one or the other. One challenge was a little boy who was more interested in *eating* the Elmer's glue than using it! Even something as common as Elmer's glue had to be rationed since it had been brought from the States!

have only been from the Holy Spirit, "We are worshiping the Living God and you have shown great disrespect to us by interrupting our service." To my utter surprise, he began to walk backwards towards the gate. He apologized for interrupting and, just as quickly as the courtyard had filled up with all these men, they disappeared. From that day on, we had no problems with the neighbors regarding our worship services. On reflecting upon that incident, I learned several things about ministering in a Muslim land. First, the more of the culture and language that you know, the better. I am convinced that because I spoke to the ringleader in his mother tongue, he was deeply affected. Second, I learned how important it is to understand that we are in a spiritual battle and being strong in the Lord is our best response to particular attacks. I felt the Holy Spirit came to my rescue and gave me what to say. I saw firsthand what Jesus meant when He said, "Do not be anxious about how you should defend yourself or what you should say, for the Holy Spirit will teach you in that very hour what you ought to say." (Luke 12:12) My faith deepened, and I had courage to trust the leading of the Holy Spirit.

Tat Preaching in the German Lutheran Church in Tehran, 1979

On Sunday, November 4, 1979, Patty and our children and I were at what then was called the "Ghavam Saltaneh" Church, now known as St. Peters. We had arrived early for the 6 p.m. worship service, so our kids were playing in the garden. We were passing the time enjoying fellowshipping with some of the Christians who lived on the church grounds. Someone casually asked of us, "Have you heard what happened at the American Embassy? It has been overrun by students who call themselves followers of Ayatollah Khomeini." At first it did not strike me as a serious breach of International protocol as I was certain the police would arrive and disperse the rebellious students. After the worship service, we visited in the garden with other members, enjoying Iranian tea and sweets. We then packed into our car to head for home. It happened that the American Embassy was between the church and our home, so I suggested to Patty that we should drive by and see what was going on. We quickly saw they had blocked off the street in front of the Embassy, so we couldn't get close enough to see anything. Later that evening, we were listening to the BBC and learned that the American Embassy had been breached — the

American diplomats had been taken hostage. We were shocked! What would this mean for us and the other Americans in our church? Would we also be taken hostage? We kept a low profile for a few days and listened daily to the BBC radio broadcast, which seemed to be the best source of news concerning the Tehran situation. Khomeini's address to the nation was broadcast all over Iran, in which he announced Iran would "cut off the arm of America." We knew he meant he was going to end American support of the Shah and the influence that America had on Iran. To our relief, he also added that Iran had no problem with the people of America but only with its evil government. He added, to our relief, "Do not cut off a single hair from the heads of Americans in our country!" We gradually resumed our daily activities, not knowing how long the hostages would be held.

As we approached American Thanksgiving, I made plans to have a service for the dozen or so Americans who attended Community Church. The day before Thanksgiving, our home phone rang. It was CBS News wanting to know if we would be having a Thanksgiving Day service and could they attend it and record it for broadcast[10]. As I contemplated seeing TV trucks pulling up in front of the German church, causing a crowd to gather, and the subsequent commotion, I began to doubt the wisdom of CBS attending our service. But they assured me they would come in a taxi and there would only be two of them. I relented. The next day, we gathered for the Thanksgiving service and CBS's camera was rolling. After the service, they briefly interviewed Patty, our son Timmy, and me. Emily had a sudden attack of shyness, so was not in the filming. In that interview, we spoke highly of the kindness of the Iranian people and that we were not afraid. Then Timmy was asked, "Do you have anything you want to say?" He said, "Hi Grandma." But when we later listened to it, his words were muffled in such a way that it was unclear whether he had said "Grandpa" or "Grandma." It turned out to be a truly diplomatic thing, since the two Grandpas thought Tim's greeting was for them and the two Grandmas thought it was for *them*! Bragging rights all around as they told everyone they knew!

We had not realized it at first but the Iranian government had blocked all international calls to the U. S. Thus when the news of the hostage crisis hit the American media, our families back home became worried for they had been trying to call us to no avail. As time went by, they were

---

10. They had planned to come to *our* apartment after the service to film a traditional Thanksgiving dinner! As Patty looked at our dining table covered with piles of laundry (the dryer had broken down) and made a mental note of what food we could prepare — frozen orange juice and mushroom soup — she begged to have someone more prepared host a gathering! Food shortages were severe. An American teacher, Merilee Robertson, had already planned a very good meal, complete with a turkey, so the news crew went to her home instead.

becoming even more anxious about the situation, although we knew we were safe and were not experiencing the same level of stress. Therefore, when many of our family and friends turned on their televisions the morning of Thanksgiving Day and saw the broadcast of our interview in Tehran, they were greatly relieved. In the weeks following, we received a flood of letters from friends all over the States writing about how that Thanksgiving had been one of the happiest Thanksgivings they could ever remember because they had learned we were safe. We were overjoyed, knowing that God had been looking out for us once again and that He was in full control of our lives. God's Word once again brought comfort to us as we read, "It is the Lord who goes before you. He will be with you; He will not leave you or forsake you. Do not fear or be dismayed." (Deut. 31:8)

Soon after Thanksgiving, our mission considered it wise for me to send my family out of the country to ensure their safety. I sent Patty and our children to London to stay with my sister and her family for a while to see what would happen next. I remember taking them to the airport and standing there with my children clinging to my legs. They did not want to let go of me, but I tried to be strong. My heart was breaking as I kissed Patty and them goodbye. The drive back to our apartment was one of the loneliest moments in my life, but worsened as I opened the door to our home and walked into a silent apartment. The days crawled by and my loneliness progressively got worse. Finally, the news announced that Ayatollah Taleghani had died and there would be several days of mourning; all shops would be closed. I was advised not to go out at all for several days. All I had was a shortwave radio to listen to the news, a TV that received only one channel that broadcast readings from the Quran all day, and a phone. The highlight of any day was to have a call from Patty in London. One night when the electricity was out and I was sitting in the dark, the phone rang; it was Patty. I could tell from her voice that things were not going well in her world in London. Apparently, my sister Peggie's two children, as well as my two, were very sick with the flu —to add to the situation, they only had one bathroom! The conditions now

Lutheran Church courtyard in Tehran, 1979

were hard on all of them and I felt I had to do something about it. I assured her I would do my best to come as soon as possible. When I hung up the phone, a dark cloud of depression settled over me. I felt totally unable to help Patty, I was dying of loneliness, and worse, God was nowhere to be found. As I sat in the dark, I felt myself sinking deeper into despair. Almost like a drowning man who comes up for one more breath of air before it is too late, I yelled, "Jesus, help me!" At that very moment, a verse flashed before my eyes:

"No temptation (or trial) has overtaken you that is not common to man. God is faithful and he will not let you be tempted beyond your ability, but with the temptation he will also provide the way of escape, that you may be able to endure it." (I Corinthians 10:13)

As I opened my Bible and reread these words, there was a flicker of hope in me. For the first time in many nights, I slept better. I sensed God had released me from my church responsibilities and I quickly received permission from the church board to join Patty and our children in London. I realized how easy it was for me to be overtaken by my circumstances and how delinquent I had been in leaning on Jesus, my Lord. This experience was a way that God welded a truth to my heart and enabled me to shepherd many others through the years with the same truth. Glory to God, who gives us the victory in Christ and the wisdom to know how to depend upon Him!

I arrived in London in early December on an Iran Air jumbo jet. I was a happy passenger since I was on my way to see my family. They served a wonderful Iranian dish, chelo kebab, and I fellowshipped with a few other Iranian passengers. As we left Iranian airspace, the women on board made their way to the restroom to change out of their Islamic clothes, emerging in some of Europe's finest fashions. When my turn to go through passport control at Heathrow came, the officer looked up at me with a stunned look, seeing that I was an American. He apologized for the long wait, since they had cleared the hall from all other flights to accommodate my flight from Iran. "I don't mind," I said. "I stand with the people of Iran."

What a joyous reunion it was with Patty and our children! I was so grateful for how Peggie and Andrew had hosted my family until I would be able to get there. The hostage crisis continued, and it was almost Christmas. We had to go standby on a Pan Am flight to New York. The Lord opened the way, and we arrived in Denver, Colorado, to the excited welcoming by Patty's family. The first thing I felt after living in Iran was a release from the anxiety of having lived in Iran as an American that first year of the Revolution.

While home, we discovered that Emily, Tim, and Patty all needed surgeries of various kinds. Our daughter Emily had suffered from repeated bladder infections several years before we had moved to Tehran. While we were home in the States, we took her to a renowned urologist who soon diagnosed her problem. Whenever her bladder contracted, urine would be forced back into her kidneys because of a birth defect that left her with poorly functioning ureters, which caused a backflow of urine into her kidneys. The doctor explained that he would surgically repair the valve. He said it would be a serious surgery and possibly incredibly painful. "It has been known to make grown men cry." Emily was a small four-year-old! Patty's terror was met by a verse the Lord gave her that day: "He will carry His lambs in His arms and gently lead their mothers." (Isaiah 40:11). Tearfully, she agreed to the surgery. It was a nine-day hospital stay, incredibly difficult at times, but Emily was a brave little patient! Since then, she has not had any after-effects. Later we learned that the wonderful doctor retired not long afterwards, and if we had not come home when we had, we would not have benefited from his years of experience. Once again, we were witnesses to God's gracious provisions for my family. Tim and Patty both underwent urological surgeries as well. It was a Christmas we will never forget!

The time came to return to Iran, even though the hostage crisis was still unresolved. However, our fellow missionaries in Iran informed us that life had returned to "normal," so it would be safe to return. On February 5, 1980, we flew back to Iran. The day we arrived, a light snow had fallen in Tehran, making it look so clean and bright. Soon we were back to our weekly schedule, leading worship on Friday mornings in the German Church.

I always loved springtime in Tehran, because it was when all of Iran began to prepare for their NoRuz (New Year) celebrations. Everyone seemed to awaken from a long winter's nap and the streets seemed to burst at their seams as people began their preparations for the New Year. Every home set up a "haft-seen" table, a table of Seven S's which could include any of the following:

- **Sabzeh** — wheat or lentils grown in a tray or dish prior to NoRuz to represent rebirth,
- **Samanu** — a sweet pudding made from wheat germ, symbolizing material blessings
- **Senjed** — the dried fruit of the lotus tree which represents love,
- **Seer** — garlic, which represents healing
- **Seeb** — apple, which represents beauty and health,
- **Somaq** — sumac berries, which represent the color of the sunrise and new opportunity
- **Serkeh** — vinegar, which represents age and maturity
- **Sonbol** — the hyacinth flower with its strong fragrance heralding the coming of spring, and transformation
- **Sekkeh** — coins representing prosperity and success

I have taken these symbols from time to time and used them as a basis of a New Year's sermon series. In a way, they express the deep longings of the Iranian heart which ultimately only God can fulfill in Christ.

The shops at NoRuz stock up on sweets, nuts, and live goldfish (which become part of the decoration on the haft-seen tables). It is a season when many spring clean, put a fresh coat of paint on the walls in their homes, and have their Persian carpets cleaned. It is customary to purchase new clothes. For the two weeks of NoRuz, it is as if life stands still. People take off from work and welcome visitors daily. It is one long break from the doldrums of life. On the thirteenth day after NoRuz (Seezdah-be-Dar), everyone leaves their homes and goes on a picnic. Some have suggested it is bad luck to stay home on the thirteenth day of the New Year. Whatever the reason behind this tradition, it is pretty much universally celebrated by Iranians, wherever they are in the world.

Not wanting to be left out, in the spring of 1980, Patty, Tim, Emily and I were invited to join Richard and Doreen Corley and a few other Iranian friends on a ride to the countryside hoping to find a nice place for a picnic. On the outskirts of Tehran, we came to a beautiful garden surrounded by a low wall. Before I could protest, Richard Corley had climbed over the wall and invited us all to follow. We encountered several other groups in the garden who were also celebrating, but in the spirit of the day, no one seemed offended that we had breached their wall without an invitation. Everyone seemed to enjoy the day.

The Corleys played a very important role in our lives the year we lived in Tehran. They were active members of the Community Church, so we saw them almost weekly. But their greatest help to us came when they invited us to their home on Wednesdays for a time of prayer and fellowship. Patty and I often arrived at their home stressed and fearful about our future in Iran. They, on the other hand, always greeted us with confidence and peace. Their home became a refuge for us as they helped us refocus on God's sovereignty and the assurance of His promise never to leave us or forsake us.

As Easter approached, the State Department began to call us regularly. At first, they were urging us to leave Iran as soon as possible. When they realized we were planning to stay until God showed us when we should leave, they became more understanding. They now wanted to know if I would take communion to the American hostages. The thought of any interaction with the students holding the American hostages was not one that I welcomed. But because they persisted, I reluctantly agreed on the condition that the Iranian government would lend their support to the idea. I knew the State Department was desperate to have contact with someone who had had eyes on the hostages and could report how they were doing. In the end, the Iranian government did not like the suggestion. (An Iranian pastor eventually was allowed a visit with the hostages, but I do not know if he was able to give a report to the State Department.)

Anxieties were building, and there was a palpable tension in the air. We were all waiting with bated breath to see how the current political events would affect our lives and ministry.

NO STRANGER

CHAPTER NINE
THE NEXT GENERATION

Revolutions are like earthquakes! There are tremors that change the landscape; the aftershocks then follow. The Revolution in Iran resulted from many groups working together to overthrow a common enemy: the Shah. While I believe the Shah had begun his rule with the noble goal of bringing Iran into the modern era, over time many things went wrong. He began to fear all opposition, so he formed his secret service, "Savak," growing in power and regularly eliminating his enemies. There is a reason that kings throughout history tolerated their opposition by giving them a public voice, thereby weakening their power. But Mohammad Reza Shah Pahlavi would not tolerate any voice of opposition. As the demand for oil in the west grew and the price continued to rise, the Shah's power increased; along with a growing corruption in his administration. In 1963, a little-known cleric by the name of Rouhollah Khomeini led a demonstration against the government. Patty and I were high school students at Community School and, ironically, we were studying the French Revolution. We found it exciting and yet terrifying to hear gunfire in the streets and see the devastation that the street mobs were causing in Tehran. It was after this first earthquake that the Shah banished Khomeini to Iraq where his disdain for the Shah grew more with each passing day. Later, Saddam Hussein banished him to France. I have often wondered how much of Khomeini's drive to destroy the Shah was more about a personal vendetta than a philosophical disagreement. Had it been more about revenge and power than high spiritual hopes for Iran?

Although Khomeini appeared to be the face of the revolt against the Shah, it was actually made up of coalitions of opposing groups. These groups formed a united front against the Shah and his government, which was based on a belief that all the groups would have a seat at the political table. When Khomeini arrived in Tehran, everyone rallied around him, and for a few months there was unprecedented freedom. Many groups gathered in front of the University of Tehran and distributed their propaganda, hoping to garner support. Alongside these groups were Christians distributing Christian literature. There was a feeling of euphoria in the air. But by the fall of 1979, Khomeini showed his true intentions. He sent his thugs to the campus of the University of Tehran to shut down every group that was in opposition to him. Those who opposed him were badly beaten. Our home was near to the hospital locally referred to as "Hospital of One Thousand Beds" because of its being the largest hospital in Tehran. During the crackdown led by Khomeini's followers, the sound of ambulance sirens day and night bringing wounded and dying students to the hospital were heard. I later learned that hundreds of parents and family members stormed the hospital demanding to know where their wounded family members were. It was a harrowing time to be a college student at the University of Tehran.

Tat and Family in Tehran, 1979

Months later, when all opposition had been crushed, the people of Iran were asked to vote on establishing the Islamic Republic of Iran, over which Khomeini appointed himself as "velayat-e- Fagih" (The Guardian of the Jurist), in essence making him the final authority over the government of Iran and thus establishing a modern-day theocracy. His voice would be the very voice of God.

How did these turbulent events affect the national church of Iran? I am sure many wiser than I can answer this question better but because I was living in Iran at the time, I trust that some of my observations will add value to the discussion on this topic that most likely will continue for many years to come. As I have already written, Patty and I arrived in Iran to assume the responsibility of pastoring the Community Church of Tehran in July 1979, just five months after Khomeini had made his dramatic return to Iran. The first thing that became clear to all of us was that any association with America was now taboo, for as far as the Revolutionary guard were concerned, he was no more than a puppet of America. American flags were trampled on and burned at every opportunity. President Carter was burned in effigy. What kind of effect did this have on the Persian church? It presented a problem for the Evangelical Church because they received financial help from America and now had a brand-new American missionary to deal with.

It had been made very clear that I was in Iran to be the pastor of the American Community Church, which had been decimated by the sudden evacuation of over 50,000 Americans. The Persian church could now take a deep breath and hope that my arrival would not add to the growing list of challenges they were facing and would face from the new Islamic regime. With this in mind, I was asked if I would serve as a youth advisor to the four sister congregations in Tehran, to which I enthusiastically agreed. After all, I had returned to Iran not to minister to Western Christians but to serve the Iranian church, of which I felt I had been a member since childhood. The Evangelical church of Iran, having been patterned after the Presbyterian church in America, consisted of three Presbyteries under a Synod. What is unique to Iran was that the three Presbyteries were organized based on the language spoken by each. There were two Farsi- speaking congregations, one Armenian-speaking congregation, and one Assyrian-language church. Each one worshiped in their native language, but Farsi was the national language that everyone had to know. When I visited the Armenian congregation, I taught in Farsi since that was the language everyone held in common.

In many ways, things had not changed on the street level of life in Tehran. The storefronts around St. Peters were packed with shoppers, the streets were clogged with cars, and church members from all backgrounds attended services. I visited our mission offices at Ghavam-o-Saltaneh once a week to pick up our mail, which was delivered to a P.O. Box; I often stuck my head into the offices of the Iranian Bible Society and even the offices of the Synod of the Evangelical church. They often invited me in for a cup of tea and a visit. On Sundays, I drove my family to the church and was allowed to drive my car into the church compound.

Every visit to St. Peter's brought back special memories. Years ago, when I was in sixth grade, the Community Church of Tehran met there on Sunday mornings. All of us kids from the Boarding School would parade in and fill an entire pew. Sometimes I sat next to Patty. I took my first communion there and learned the spiritual discipline of listening to sermons I did not understand. Mercifully, the services ended promptly on time so we could be released to run out into the beautiful grounds and play with our friends. Years later, when I was in eleventh grade, I lived with a fellow student in a former missionary residence that had been turned into several apartments. It was a lonely time, as there was not much to do but study. I had a radio and often listened to Armed Forces Radio. The highlight of the week was when they played a countdown of the top rock and roll songs from the States. We took our meals at the guest house, which allowed us to meet interesting people traveling through Iran. The mission van provided us with our transportation to Community School. It was on these grounds that I met some heroes of Presbyterian mission work in Iran. I had several encounters with Dr. John Elder. His brilliant white hair intrigued me. Later I would delight in mining through his book, Biblical Approach to the Muslim, for wonderful nuggets of wisdom for my own ministry. I visited the austere room, which Dr. William McElwee Miller called home and was impressed with his lack of interest in material comforts; his passion was for books. His writing would also inform me about what a Christian's response should be to Islam and I was spellbound in reading his book: Ten Muslims Meet Christ. It is often in hindsight that one realizes the life-shaping impact others have on us along life's way. I now realize what amazing pioneers in Muslim evangelism these men were and how in many ways it was their lives and ministries that set the groundwork for the great awakening that we are witnessing in these days.

One day when I went to pick up my mail, I noticed three letters: one from a friend in Egypt and two from friends in America. I remember it had been a very anxious time of wondering about our future in Iran; but when I opened these letters, I was confronted again with the truth that our lives were in the hands of our sovereign Heavenly Father. All three letters had the same verse from Psalm 91:11— "For He will command His angels concerning you to guard you in all his ways." I was overwhelmed by the fact that three letters from three different places in the world conveyed the same message! It was a direct message from God, I was convinced. Who else could have engineered this? Needless to say, we were greatly encouraged and blessed by those letters. I cherished the words in my heart and counted on God to be our refuge and strength.

One of my initial responsibilities was to serve as an advisor to the youth and to attend their meetings. Now, no one had told me that when a pastor attends a meeting, it is expected that he should be prepared to preach a message. I thought I could just slip in the back and observe what was going on. On the contrary, as soon as I appeared at the door, they all stood up and each young person greeted me with a warm handshake. They immediately turned the meeting over to me. It was not a large group, and they were friendly, but my ability to speak Farsi was still weak and I had not prepared anything. Instead, I shared my testimony, which they all seemed to like. The next time they invited me back to the same group at St. Peters, I had prepared a message. Preparing a short Bible message was not that difficult for me, but preparing to share it in Farsi was another story. I had spent hours looking up words in the dictionary and had finally prepared a fifteen-minute message. After all, every time I had spoken to American youth groups, fifteen minutes seemed to be the maximum that I could hold their attention. I was quite proud that I now had a message and was ready to preach to the group. I stumbled through that lesson and everyone seemed happy to hear what I had to say. When I had finished, one of the more outspoken brothers said, "Is that all you have to say? We need more!" When had a youth group ever told me they wanted to hear more? I now knew I was in trouble. I was going to have to work much harder at preparing deeper and longer messages. Then it occurred to me that these kids were living through one of the most transformative times in the history of their country and they had to be under great duress worrying about their future. They were standing on a fault line of a historical earthquake. The foundations of their lives were being shaken. No wonder they wanted to know more about God and where they could find assurance for their future. All of a sudden, my heart filled with a significant burden for the Christian youth of Iran. What kind of future were they facing? Would the church be able to communicate a sound Biblical view of who God was and would it sustain them as they navigated their unknown future? Years later, I learned that the generation that was born and raised in the Islamic Revolution was called "The Burned-out Generation." I now knew why God had brought me to Iran at such a time.

After teaching my first lesson, I was hopeful I could do it again. In fact, they invited me to another youth group north of the city at Emmanuel

Church[11], which was another Farsi-speaking congregation. The vision for the church had come from Dr. William Miller many years earlier. I reviewed my notes and was relieved, knowing I would do a better job the second time I delivered the message. I did not know what disaster was awaiting me. When I walked into the room, a much larger group of well-dressed young people all stood out of respect for me. As I surveyed my audience, my heart nearly stopped. Half of the young people there were from St. Peter's Church where I had just been the week before! They had all decided to follow me wherever I was teaching. I was honored but also embarrassed that they would have to hear the same message I had delivered to them. But they were all so gracious. "You did a much better job the second time," one student exclaimed, hoping to encourage me. These initial experiences with the youth of the Evangelical church were just the beginning of many wonderful friendships that have lasted a lifetime.

I formed one such friendship during the early days of our time in Iran. We had the honor of getting to know the Bishop of the Anglican Church, Bishop Dehqani-Tafti. We met him in a little village in the foothills overshadowed by the majestic Mount Damavand. The name of the village was Fasham. Miss Jane Doolittle, a lifelong missionary to Iran, had a small cabin in this mountain hideaway. It was nestled next to a stream rushing with cold water from the melting snows that provided the delicious water for the city of Tehran. Tehran is hot in the summer so we welcomed the invitation to visit Miss Doolittle, whom we had known since our youth. Upon arrival, we crossed the stream and found that Miss Doolittle had other company. We were introduced to Bishop Dehqani. Over a delicious snack of tea and sweets, we sat and listened in to what the Bishop was sharing. We quickly learned about the extreme pressures the Anglican Church was undergoing.

That first year after the Islamic Revolution, Bishop Dehqani and the Anglican Church endured more than their share of hardship. There was an assassination attempt on his life, from which God miraculously spared him. On May 6th 1980, Bahram Dehqani-Tafti, a BBC reporter and beloved teacher and the only son of Bishop Dehqani, was driving home when his car was forced off the road. He was taken and driven to a deserted area near Evin Prison where he was shot and killed. Bahram's mother, Margaret, was the daughter of British missionaries, so Bahram grew up

---

11. Also referred to as "Niloo" because it is located on Niloo Street in central Tehran.

speaking perfect English. Bahram's murder was certainly designed to send a powerful message to the Bishop: that there was no place in the future of Iran for a Muslim convert Bishop. His death also sent a broader message to the Farsi-speaking Christians in Iran that they would not be tolerated in the Islamic Republic of Iran, which sent fear into the Christian community. Many have wondered why the Anglican Church was targeted by the Islamic regime, since the other Protestant churches did not receive the same hostility. What I remember hearing those days was that it was because the Bishop was a Muslim convert who had not changed his name to reflect his conversion, maintaining his former Muslim name, which irritated the Islamic leaders. He also was very outspoken about his rights as a citizen of Iran and stood toe-to-toe with them. He was courageous and strong in his faith and resisted them. This was intolerable because in Islam anyone who converts is a reprobate and must be punished. The other denominations were led by Armenian pastors, so they were protected from the ire of the new government. In time, all Christian churches would come under attack and eventually be closed to anyone from a Muslim background.

Bahram's funeral was held at the St. Peter's Anglican Church in Tehran. I found my way into a large hall filled with people. I was first struck by the women in black chadors (a head to toe black cloth covering which Shiite Muslim women in Iran wear; a woman would never leave her home without it) and soon realized that many Muslims were there because of their love for Bahram. Bishop Dehqani had been advised to leave Iran, so he was not present. The part of the service that stood out most, as though it were yesterday, was when a poem that the Bishop had written was read aloud. Contrary to Muslim funerals calling for revenge, the Bishop described how his losing his son and the pain associated with that reminded him of the pain that God the Father must have endured in seeing His own Son crucified on the cross. As the poem was being read, I felt the Holy Spirit sweeping through the packed hall; I was aware of the sound of weeping. I'm certain that much of that sorrow was for the personal pain of loss, but it also seemed to me that our Lord was in our midst touching hearts with the power that was on display throughout the Dehqani family. Heaven will unveil how many of those women in black chadors were touched by the Gospel, for our Sovereign Heavenly Father was once again turning that which was intended for evil into that which would advance His kingdom and bring to light His glory. The Holy Spirit deeply touched me, and I came away with a deeper understanding of God's grace and a renewed passion to share my faith with my Muslim friends. (Years later, Bishop Dehqani wrote a book about his trials called <u>The Hard Awakening.</u>)

Another treasured friendship was with the Rev. Petros Sobhani. Sobhani was the pastor of the Emmanuel Church that year. He took me under his wing and coached me on how to minister to his flock. I learned much about how to be more culturally sensitive, a lesson that would serve me well in years to come as I learned how to minister to Iranians effectively. I accompanied him on several occasions as he visited members of his church, often bringing small gifts with him to give to his flock. He was very gracious and kind and was well-versed in his Bible, and loved to talk about the years that he had spent with Dr. Miller and how much he had learned from him. He reminded me of how Dr. Miller would invite his closest disciples to live with him in the Garden of Evangelism[12] (Baghe Besharat) and how they would not only study the Bible together but also learn how to live consistently with their new profession, behaving with dignity and self-respect. I was impressed with the investment of time that Dr. Miller had made with a select group of men and wondered how many other missionaries had actually devoted that time to other Iranian believers. It must have made an important impact on me, as years later, when I began to minister to them, I always sought to spend time living with them whenever possible. The Iranians have a saying, "if you really want to get to know someone take a trip with them," and I would add, "or live with them for a while."

Shortly thereafter, Rev. Sobhani asked me to assume the leadership of his youth group. A Persian youth group usually consisted of teenagers and young adults who are not yet married, very unlike my experience of youth work having been with high school students. What I soon discovered was that the Revolution had scattered his youth group, so we had to regroup. Many young people attended church, but there was not much of a ministry designed for them. I agreed to begin one, and we set Friday afternoons as the time to meet. I led worship at Community Church in the mornings and then in the late afternoon drove to Emmanuel Church. At that first meeting, we had only eight in attendance. We sang praise songs led by one girl who played the guitar, and I struggled to teach a short lesson with my broken Farsi. We prayed, asking God to bring others to join us. Over time, our group grew to over sixty young people. For much

---

12. Dr. Miller bought this garden with his own money.

of that year, my ministry consisted of giving leadership to this group, but on several occasions, I was invited to speak to the larger and more active youth groups of the Assyrian Presbyterian Church and the Armenian Presbyterian Church.

Attending the church summer conferences had always been eagerly anticipated by the young people. The Revolution had put such gatherings on hold, but now there was renewed hope that we might be able to resume them. In consultation with other churches, we began by organizing a planning committee of key leaders who agreed to meet regularly with me for planning and prayer. I look back on those days as being perhaps one of the most important contributions I made. I wish I could remember everyone who had been a part of that group, but I do remember that Florence EsHaq played a very critical role; also, Dr. Shahram Habib-Zadeh (MD) and Diba Bet-Daniel were a great help to me. The conference was planned for mid-June in 1980. I had also lined up many family and friends in America to be praying for revival for the youth of the church.

Prior to the conference, Dr. Shahram and I spent a day in the Garden of Evangelism making the necessary preparations. The wall in the front of the garden had collapsed and had been replaced by a temporary metal one. We decided it needed to be painted, so we spent several hours painting it. Then we swept out the dorm rooms, which were basically mud floors, and we were soon covered in dust. What a precious time I had with Dr. Shahram! We had become good friends and his joyful spirit was contagious. He often came to my office, bringing stacks of letters that he had received from those who were responding to the Bible correspondence course so we prayed over them asking God to pour out His Spirit on them. One day, when he came by for a visit, he seemed uncharacteristically distressed. He soon opened up to share with me his deep concern for his sister, Shiva, who was in prison. They had incarcerated her for having been active in the communist party. He pleaded, "Can we pray for her?" "Yes, of course!" Years later, I learned she had had a dream of Christ in prison not long after that, and had given her heart to the Lord. Several years afterwards, she was released from prison, no longer an advocate for communism but rather a warrior for Christ. God had uniquely prepared her for a new life of teaching and disciple making. In the late 1990s, I was asked to teach a class on discipleship for a special gathering of leaders from the Evangelical Church of Iran. The conference was held in a lovely ocean side community on the island of Cyprus. It had been over twenty years since I had been in Iran and many of the participants at this conference were of a completely different generation than the one I had known while in Iran. But to my delight, Shiva was there. I listened as she led morning devotions and was so impressed with her maturity and spiritual insights. One does not always have the joy of seeing the results of their prayers, but tears filled my eyes as I remembered huddling together in prayer with her brother in my office in Tehran. God, you are so faithful and worthy of praise!

As Patty, Timmy, Emily, and I drove into the Garden of Evangelism compound for the conference, we sensed excitement in the air as campers were arriving not only from Tehran but Mashhad, Shiraz, and Isfahan. There was the usual confusion regarding housing, but there was joy and love in the air. We faced several immediate challenges. There was one cold shower for 97 campers and a few staff. There was a swimming pool, which was helpful; but feeding this crowd presented us with a more difficult challenge. Since there were food shortages in the city, we were not allowed to buy many items in large quantities. Often, I got up early with one of the brothers to go to several bread shops just to buy enough bread for breakfast. Then if the cook wanted chickens, we had to send several people to different butcher shops to find enough for all the campers. Despite those challenges, God always provided enough food for everyone.

Patty Leading Music for the Young People in the Garden of Evangelism (Dick Corley, far right)

As the conference progressed, I soon realized it was unlike any other conference I had directed. The campers loved the Bible study times. I had prepared lessons from the Gospel of Mark and the Epistle of Romans. We formed small groups and dove into God's Word. When the time for recreation came, there was resistance because they wanted to keep studying God's Word! There were prolonged times of prayer and it was inspiring to see what God was doing. I had divided the camp into teams and had various competitions, such as finding Bible verses. We called it the Injili (Evangelical) Olympics. I introduced a scavenger hunt, which was unfamiliar to most. I informed them they had to find the largest pair of shoes in the camp. Needless to say, at size 13, I had to give up the shoes I was wearing! Patty was a real hit, since she was the only one in the camp who could touch her nose with her tongue. During one particular event, I noticed a lot of the campers were cheating and ruining the game. Uncharacteristically, I became angry and ordered them to their rooms with Bible verses to memorize about telling the truth. Despite my indignation, they survived my rebukes and there was a better spirit among them.

Conferences for Iranian Christian young people after the Revolution had many blessings. It was a time to fellowship with others from the other churches in Tehran, as well as with believers who had come from other cities. But even more important for their future was the opportunity to meet other believers of the opposite sex in a controlled environment. I observed couples sitting together talking and wondered if a marriage would be imminent. I also wondered how many marriages through the years were initiated in the Garden of Evangelism.

As with most conferences, the last night was the climax. As a youth leader from America, I did not believe one could have a conference without a campfire. Did it matter that it was 101 degrees? Of course not! I am sure a few people thought I had lost my mind. But the last night we gathered around a roaring campfire. I handed out index cards to each person and asked them to find a secluded place in the garden to spend time with God. They were to ask God, "What is keeping me from completely surrendering my life to You?" When God had revealed to them what that was, they were to write it on the card and return to the campfire. Over the next half hour, most had returned to the fire, and I invited them, if they were ready to completely dedicate their lives to the Lordship of Jesus and to serving Him, to cast the card in the fire. For the next twenty minutes, cards, cigarettes, and other items were cast into the fire as we sang praises to Jesus. By this time, many were on their knees, some weeping and others singing. But all 97 campers had in some way consecrated their lives to Jesus. In all my years of ministry, I have seen nothing like it. It was as if the Holy Spirit fell upon all of us. In retrospect, I have tried to analyze what occurred. Most likely it was because this was the first generation of Christian youth to experience life under the Islamic regime in Iran, so there must have been much anxiety about their futures.

Amidst all these fears, however, the conference attendees were finding peace in Christ, the fruit of many people praying. But most of all, it was the faithfulness of God who wanted to prepare His church for what lay ahead. During the prosperous 1970s, the Injili church had grown stagnant and desperately in need of revival. God once again used the hardships of history to bring back His people to Himself. What began in the Garden of Evangelism in the summer of 1980 overflowed into the churches in the months and years to come. These young people returned to their churches with a fire in their hearts for Christ that could not be quenched. They led worship, they preached, they witnessed, and made disciples. To this day, we are seeing the fruit of what God began in the Garden of Evangelism. It is difficult to express how grateful to God I am that Patty and I could witness this revival and to have had a small part in it. It profoundly changed our lives. We had seen God at work and we were hungry to see more.

The history of Iran has often been described as a contest between the dynasties and the Islamic clerics. Sometimes the Kings of Iran subdued the power of the clerics. Reza Shah, the founder of the Pahlavi dynasty, was well known for his disdain for the chador and other symbols of Islam. Chadors (veils) were, in his view, counter to national progress, and Reza Shah frequently ordered his soldiers to rip them off the women to humiliate them. Since the Revolution of 1979, the chador became a symbol of the Revolution. When it became clear that Iran was being transformed from its western cultural bent, thus returning to the time of the chador, the women of Iran began to fear what lay ahead. They knew they would be counted as half a man legally, that many of the freedoms they had enjoyed would be stripped away, that their husbands would have the legal right to their children and that they would not be issued a passport to travel abroad without their husband's permission. They saw their freedoms slipping away and there was great unrest among the higher-class women of Iran. Many chose to leave the country rather than to put up with the humiliation that was being thrust upon them.

CHAPTER TEN
GO HOME!

    The conference was now behind us, so we were free to focus on what our future in Iran would be. The hostage crisis was dragging on, and the hostages had been moved to a new location. In July 1980, we were facing the one-year anniversary of our arrival in Iran. The normal procedure was for our mission to send our passports to the police station and to have our residence permits renewed for a nominal fee. They assured us it was all a matter of routine and not to worry. The following day, we received a call from our mission office informing me I was to appear in person at an Iranian government official's office. The mission asked a member of the Iranian church who was a lawyer to accompany me. He was a believer from a Jewish background, so there would be no risk of his being accused of being a Muslim convert. We arrived on time and were ushered into a waiting room and offered tea. There seemed to be little activity in the office, but when we asked when our appointment would be, we were informed that the deputy in charge had not yet arrived. Appointments in Iran are not as punctual as they are in the States, so it wasn't unusual to have to wait. Many glasses of tea later, around noon, I was called in to stand before a bearded man dressed in gray, sitting behind an enormous desk. "Passports," he barked in perfect English. I respectfully handed him our passports. He glanced through them and without even looking up, he announced, "We have orders from above to ask you to leave Iran. You have ten days to depart!" He returned our passports.

    "Sir, may I say something?" I blurted out with as much respect as I could muster. "What is it?" Now he was actually looking at me. "I just wanted to inform you why we have been in your beloved country. We came here because we love your people and we love your land. We came to share the love of God with them. Also, I want you to know our God instructs us to respect government leaders and to obey them, so we will do our best to leave Iran as you have instructed." Then I added, "I also want you to know that we are in no way associated with the government of America. We represent the Christians of America." I was quite pleased with myself, but he was not at all impressed. Then I asked one more question: "How am I going to find tickets on any airline within the next ten days?" "Don't worry, Iran Air will make room for you." With those parting words, I was ushered out of his office. I said goodbye to my lawyer friend and stood there for a moment in shock.

As I descended the steps of the government offices, I tried to process what had just taken place. I was being ordered to leave Iran. I had come to Iran to live and serve its people and share the love of God. It had been only a year ago that Patty and I had sold all our belongings in America and moved to Iran with our children. We had said goodbye to our families and our country and now we were told we had to pack up and return home. I had just begun to see my ministry starting to grow, and I even had an invitation to preach at St. Peter's Church in August of that year. It felt like a bad dream. How could God let this happen? How would Patty feel about leaving? How would the members of the Community Church react to the news that the church would be closed? I thought about all the young people that I had been working with and wondered how this news would affect them? Many of their kind faces flashed before my mind's eye and I feared it would be very hard for them to say goodbye to Patty and me. I felt a panic attack brewing, but gradually I was able to bring my emotions under control. I could tangibly feel the presence of the Lord, which brought His comfort and assurance that He was in control of the whole situation.

Time seemed to stand still as I stood on the sidewalk, but then somewhere back in the hidden resources of my mind a thought was born: *If as an American citizen you are in trouble and you do not have an American Embassy, go to the Swiss Embassy and ask for help.* Here I was in the middle of Islamic Iran and the Revolutionary students had captured my embassy, so I took a taxi to the Swiss Embassy. The ride there seemed to take forever. Seeing the Swiss flag comforted me since I was greatly in need of a friend. I rang the doorbell and was escorted inside; a gracious lady with a thick French accent asked me how she could help. She listened attentively as I explained my plight. "Let me inform the Ambassador and see what he can do." After a quick call to the Ambassador, she led me down a hall and opened a large black door and suddenly I was standing in front of another large desk; this time, however, a very gentle man asked me, "How can I help you?" I showed him our passports and explained my situation. "I am afraid I won't be able to find air passage out of Iran in time and I really do not want to fly Iran Air." The embargoes that President Carter had placed on Iran had resulted in Iran Air's struggling to find spare parts for their Boeing 747s and many of the mechanics who maintained the Iran Air fleet were Korean and had left Iran, so I was concerned for our safety. The Ambassador looked up with a smile and asked, "Which day do you want to leave?" I knew I did not want to put it off until the tenth day just in case something might go wrong and potentially get us into trouble with the Iranian government. "How about the seventh day?" That seemed the safe choice. He picked up his phone and called Swiss Air and basically told them they would have to make room for the Stewart family on the date we had agreed upon. I thanked him profusely and left his office with a new air of hope.

With airline tickets in hand, I was now faced with several painful challenges. How would I prepare my family for such a short notice departure from Iran? How would I inform the members of our church that there would be only one more worship service before the church was closed permanently? What would I do with all the files and books that belonged to the church? What were we to do with our furniture and belongings we had brought from America? How could we say goodbye to the wonderful young people of the "Injili" church with whom we had become very close friends?

When Friday arrived, we gathered in the German church for our final meeting. We celebrated communion together, and I preached from Isaiah where God says He is doing a new thing and now it springs forth (Isaiah 43:19). I was not sure how God was going to use this, but He was definitely changing our lives and that of the members of our church. We had a memorable potluck lunch together and then, with tears flowing down our faces, we said goodbye. Some of our members understood Farsi so they could find other churches, but for those who could not, there would be no more church to attend.

Now we had to dispose of our belongings. We had little time to accomplish this, so we invited our friends to come by to say goodbye and take whatever they wanted. As people were leaving our home with armfuls of household items, clothes, toys, and clothing, we soon discovered we had more friends than we had realized! The apartment was now almost empty!

What remained were the Christian books, totaling over a thousand, which I had accumulated from the many Christians who had been evacuated just before the Revolution. For the time being, they would stay in what had been my office in our home. After our departure, our apartment was rented to two Christian sisters who were very active for the Lord; during a season when there was little to no commerce between Iran and the US, these books became a great resource for them and the young people of the "Injili" Church. There were many commentaries, theological books, and biographies. Years later, these books were moved to the St. Peter's Church compound and became a part of a collection of historically valuable books. Years later, I learned how valuable those books had been for the spiritual health of the church during those difficult days.

Tat as a Pastor in Iran, 1979

Our last week in Tehran was a whirlwind of activity. I donated the Community Church Peykan station wagon to the Evangelical church. However, the most important challenge I faced was what to do with the Community Church Bank account that held a balance of $50,000 US dollars. I knew I did not want the Islamic Republic to have this money, which belonged to the Lord. I asked a good friend who was a businessman to accompany me to the bank and help me withdraw the funds in Rials (the currency of Iran). When we arrived at the bank and filled out the withdrawal forms, they informed us it would take a few hours to count it all. We finally collected the funds and put them in a large briefcase, and left. I had never seen that much money in my life and felt a great weight of responsibility. We decided to visit the major Christian ministries and donate these funds to them. We went to the Iranian Bibles Society, the Synod of the Evangelical Church, Campus Crusade, and the Garden of Evangelism, and in all, I gave away $49,000! I took a check of $1,000 to

New York with me and gave it to the Presbyterian Church (PCUSA) mission office as seed money for the new Community Church in Tehran. What is so touching about this story is that two weeks after I had distributed the funds to these ministries, President Carter put a ban on all American transfers of money to Iran. These funds provided the salaries for many Iranian Christians during those tumultuous times.

Soon after our departure, we learned that representatives of the government were posted at the doors of Protestant churches requiring all who entered for worship to show their identification cards. Because it was now illegal for a Muslim to convert from Islam, anyone with a Muslim name who wanted to attend the services would be turned away. Armenians and Assyrians were exempt from this restriction because they were not born Muslim, so if one had an Armenian or Assyrian name, they were considered a legitimate worshiper. Later on, it became common to find government representatives in the services reporting on Muslim-background believers. Some church goers reported they could hear the government two-way radios crackling during the worship services.

Persecution had come to the church.

Finally, the day came for our departure from Iran. Our flight was scheduled to depart at 8 a.m. but we were required to be at the airport at 4 a.m.! It was July 1980. Our landlord loaded our bags into his Land Rover and we followed in a taxi. We drove without headlights to avoid being detected. Timmy and Emily were groggily asleep in the backseat. When we arrived at the airport, we were surprised by more than twenty young people from the Injili church, who had spent the night at the airport fasting and praying for our trip! Some of them had read in the newspaper a few weeks earlier that there were American spies in Iran and that they would soon be expelled. They realized we were the "spies," so they were concerned that we might not be able to leave the country safely. It certainly strengthened our hearts to walk into the airport with a host of young people carrying our baggage and our children. Nothing could have prepared us for the chaos we faced upon entering the airport: it was packed with many Iranians fleeing their homeland. We had numerous checkpoints, and at one point our children and I passed through one of them, but they did not let Patty through — a very tense moment! Realizing she spoke Farsi and would not take no for an answer, they let her pass. We had to place our suitcases on a large table and open them for inspection. I had forgotten that one of the new rules was that no Persian carpets could be taken out of the country. As they opened one of our trunks, there, right on top, was a small bedside carpet I had brought to Iran just a year ago. It had been woven in our basement in Tabriz by a Muslim-background believer who could not find work, so my mother had hired him to weave carpets for each of us children. I feared now that they might take away it from us. At the very minute that the trunk was opened, and the carpet exposed, a woman across the airport began screaming, cursing the regime. She was clutching her gold jewelry as a customs agent was insisting she take it off. Because there was a thousand-dollar limit on what they could take out of the country, wealthy ladies were wearing all of their jewelry at once, hoping to sell them once out of the country. Once this lady began to scream, she drew the attention of everyone in the area, including our customs agent, who closed our trunk and never even noticed our rug. The next checkpoint was for ticket holders only, and no one else could go with us. At that point, one of the young men from a Muslim background who had been attending our youth meetings at Emmanuel Church gave me a hug and whispered in my ear, "I just wanted you to know that I have given my life to Jesus!" These were the last words I heard from my flock on Iranian soil. Tears welled up in my eyes as I praised God for His graciousness in letting me hear from this brother. It was as if God was saying to me, "Tat, go in peace, you may be leaving, but I am here to stay!"

As Patty, our children, and I passed the ticket checkpoint, we were ushered into a small room with several chairs and two men at their computers. I recognized immediately that they were the "pasdaran," members of the Revolutionary army of the Islamic Revolution. They asked for our passports to enter into their computers. Again, God showed His mercy to us, for they were speaking Turkish (so I could understand them) and trying to find some reason to fine us or delay our departure. Our children, all this time, slept on the cold tile floor, oblivious to any danger. The men grew more frustrated as they could find nothing. We had violated no Iranian laws during the time we lived in Iran, we had paid our Iranian income taxes, and we were leaving the country as ordered. Finally, in disgust, they told us to go. We thought we could relax, but one more hurdle remained. We had now arrived at our boarding gate, where we were to board a shuttle bus that would take us out to the plane. Just as we sat down in the waiting area, an announcement came over the loudspeaker, "Will the Stewart family please step out of line?" We were ordered to check with the Swiss Air desk. Patty was sure we would now be taken out and shot! I looked at Patty and could see her apprehension. Were they finally going to find a reason to fine us or keep us from leaving Iran? I nervously walked over to the airline desk, expecting to hear the worst. "Mr. Stewart, we need to make some changes to your tickets. We hope it is okay with you, but we have had to put you in First Class." I could hardly believe what I was hearing. I took a deep breath of relief and thanked them profusely. We had never before flown First Class!

As we climbed up the stairs to board the 727 Boeing plane that would take us to Zurich, Switzerland, with a connecting flight to New York, I paused and looked out over Tehran, which had been our home for the past year. There was relief that now we would be free from the control of a regime that so fiercely opposed Christianity, but also great apprehension for what our brothers and sisters in Christ would be facing. Of course, we had no way of knowing what lay ahead for them. But we knew intuitively that they were going to face difficult times. We did not know how God was going to use the Islamic Republic of Iran to fan the flames of the greatest spiritual awakening in their history. It was not until years later that I realized how we had witnessed history in the making, that we had walked the streets of Tehran as God began a new chapter in the history of Iran. God had given us front-row seats to watch the unfolding of this great "people movement" as Iranian Muslims put their faith in our Lord Jesus Christ. As time passed and I gained more perspective on all that we had witnessed during our year in Iran, I realized the year 1979 was a year in which something dramatically changed in the heavens over Iran. It was as though God opened the windows of heaven and was pouring out His Spirit in new ways upon the Iranian people. He was doing a new work in Iran! I remember my parents telling me with a great sense of disappointment how in the more than twenty years they had served in Iran, they saw only five Muslims come to Christ. In those years leading up to the Revolution, it was rare to hear about Muslims converting to Christ. Yes, there were converts, but they were few and far between. But after the Revolution, the incidents of those having dreams and visions of Christ skyrocketed. The testimonies of miraculous healings increased, and many lives were touched. There were signs and wonders that accompanied the preaching of the Word. The Lion of Judah was on the march and the gates of hell could not prevail against Him.

Arriving back in America was not without its challenges. We had not been told about some of the new laws that the Carter administration had passed. One of those laws was that Americans were not permitted to travel to Iran. When the customs agent asked us which countries we had visited, we proudly told him, "Iran." "That is impossible," he announced adamantly. He made us all get out of line while he scrambled to find some special forms that had to be filled out. We told him we had traveled to Iran before the inception of that law. We stood there weary from our long ordeal of being up the entire night before we left and all that we had been through to get out of Iran. and now wondered if our own country would let us back in. Fortunately, he found the necessary forms, and we were allowed to step back onto American soil. As we stood waiting for a taxi to take us to our hotel, my son Tim pulled at my pant leg, "Daddy, look, an American flag that's not burning!" For the past months, the only American flags we had seen were either burning or being disrespectfully trampled on. Having lived for a year in a country that had declared itself an Islamic theocracy and oppressed its people who deviated from its dictates, it certainly was a good feeling to be back in America where we could express ourselves without fear and where we had freedom to worship according to our consciences. It is ironic how it often takes losing those freedoms we take for granted in America to fully appreciate them and to want to protect them.

CHAPTER ELEVEN
WHAT NOW?

In the days following our return to America, our mission debriefed us and prepared us for re-entry into life in America. We were reminded of the graciousness of God in preserving us in a very hostile anti-American environment. They explained to us about Post-Traumatic Stress Disorder (PTSD) and how we would most likely have flashbacks to times when we had been afraid or had experienced great anxiety. We were grateful for this time to reflect on what we had so recently experienced in Iran and how it might affect us in the future. This counsel helped us understand why, for months after our return to America, Patty and I had difficulty falling asleep. Whenever I heard a car backfire, I tensed up, remembering the gunfire in the streets of Tehran. At that meeting, they informed us we would remain on salary for the next six months, during which I was to be available to speak in churches about our experiences in Iran.

Patty and I had to come to grips with all we had been through in the past year. First, we had to face the reality that what we had experienced was very traumatic and it would take some time to recover. After all, we had sold all our earthly belongings before we had moved to Tehran; we now had to start over accumulating furnishings for a new home. We had said goodbye to our American congregation and had just been settling into pastoring a new church with an entirely new set of relationships. We had been readjusting to life in Tehran and relearning Farsi. Essentially, we were back where we had begun!

Secondly, we found ourselves confronted with many unanswered questions: *Had we somehow misunderstood God's call to go to Iran? What good had our time in Iran been for the Kingdom of God?* These were momentous questions that played over and over in my mind and kept me up at night.

Thirdly, we wrestled with what our next step was to be. I felt as though the rug had just been pulled out from under us. Was God removing my call from doing ministry with Iranians? Did he want me to return to serving the American Church? It was a very perplexing time for Patty and me. As we prayed, we asked God to show us what we were to do next. The Iranian population in America at that time was much smaller than what it is at this writing, and I wondered if there was any way to fulfill our call to work with Iranians now that we were back in America?

Fourthly, we now faced an America that had become very hostile towards Iran and its people because of the hostage crisis. This raised the question: *Would I be able to find any ministries with a vision for reaching Iranians in America?* During those early days at home, I was contacted by several reporters asking me about my experience in Iran. Apparently, my answers were not the ones they were after, because they never quoted me or wrote about me. I had told them the truth: that the Iranian people had been, mostly, very gracious and helpful to us and we understood it was the regime that was hostile to America but not the Iranian people. Evidently, they wanted to hear of conflict and angry mobs, rather than peaceful coexistence. It made me question all reports I read in the papers about Iran since the media's agenda seemed to have been to stir up animosity and hatred towards Iran. That the students had taken over of the American Embassy on November 4, 1979, was the final straw that had totally humiliated the American government. This act of aggression enraged the press and thus reporters were looking for sensational stories of how Americans had been poorly treated in Iran. They were not interested in hearing about the kindness that so many Americans had experienced during those challenging days by everyday Iranians. They were also looking for any story that would fuel the anger that was brewing in the hearts of Americans, who each evening watched as Ted Koppel solemnly announced how many more days Americans had been held hostage in Iran. I chose, therefore, to avoid the American press as much as possible.

As we were confronted with our own country's hate and disdain for Iran during the hostage crisis, we were often being pulled in two directions. We could understand the frustrations that the long ordeal of the hostage crisis was causing our fellow Americans. It seemed to bring out the worst in some people. Patty once shared about our time in Iran with a member of her church and his response was that we should have "nuked them all." Patty protested, "But we were living there and we would have been killed too!" His answer: "Oh, well!" There were also several violent incidents in Colorado where we were living at the time. A couch was dropped from a second-floor balcony intended to hit an Iranian student. Thankfully, it missed him, but it raised the level of fear among Iranian students at the time. During those days, the drumbeat of hostility kept intensifying as each night America tuned in to listen to Ted Koppel's reports: "America held hostage, Day [Number]." (The crisis lasted 444 days.)

During those days, people asked us, "What was it like being an American in Iran during the hostage crisis?" We have always sought to answer that question truthfully. And our answer was that there was a mix of reactions to our presence there. There were Iranian friends, not all Christians, who were very concerned about our wellbeing. They often called to ask how we were doing and offered to help us shop for items that were hard to find in the market. They informed us which days were better to stay indoors. Some invited us to their homes. While Patty was in London during the early stages of the hostage crisis, I was invited to the home of a Muslim family of merchants in the big bazaar in Tehran. I believe they owned several fabric shops. Their son picked me up at my apartment since I did not know how to get to their home. When I walked in their front door, I noticed several semi-automatic rifles neatly stacked in the foyer. I must admit that the scene was disturbing. But they greeted me with such enthusiasm that I soon forgot what I had just witnessed. I took my shoes off, as was customary, and made my way to a comfortable couch and was served tea. Out of the corner of my eye, I saw a television on which some children were watching a children's program. I noticed the children were drawing semi-automatic guns. I thought that was a bit strange for a children's program. Then I heard the lady on the television, who was, of course, fully draped in black Islamic garb say, "Children, we are drawing these guns so that when you grow up, you can kill Americans who are the Big Satan, our number one enemy." How chilling to realize what these children, and thousands of other children in Iran, were being taught at such an impressionable age: hatred for America! At about 10 p.m. the man of the house arrived home, and dinner was served. We all called him "Hadj Agha" for he had made a pilgrimage to Mecca ("Hadj"), so literally "Sir

Hadj." Approximately twenty people gathered around a table loaded with enough delicious Iranian dishes to feed a large multitude. Hadj Agha looked at me and asked, "Are you not a Christian cleric?" "I am." "Would you please lead us in prayer for our meal?" I was not expecting that, but asked everyone to bow their heads as I explained I would be speaking with the living God. The Holy Spirit graciously led me to thank God for His love revealed to us in the life and work of Jesus Christ, and then I prayed for peace between our two nations. When I ended with "Amen," they all joined in with me. A most delicious meal with much laughter and comradeship followed.

Patty and I confronted Iranians and Americans alike who had the same spiritual problem; they had been overcome by hate. In some cases, it was prompted by empathy for the hostages and their families and disdain for the leaders of Iran. In other cases, it was spurred on by religious zeal for Islam and hate for the Shah and for any government that had supported him. Whatever the roots were, they were destructive, and it confirmed once again the need for the transforming power of the Gospel. I had tasted what could happen when I had gone into the home of fanatical Muslims, but found love and respect for me and for my faith. It gave me hope for the future of Iran and its people who were being suffocated by hatred. It gave me hope for Americans who were letting the hostage crisis lead them down their own self-destructive path of hate. Over the years, we have seen Christ at work in both Iranians and Americans. Many times, after I had spoken at an American church and shared what God was doing in Iran, American Christians would come up to me to share with me they wanted to repent of their disdain for Iran. Likewise, the hate for America that so many Iranians showed in those early years of the Revolution has melted away. Today, you will find that most Iranians love America and treasure the freedoms we enjoy.

We had nowhere to go when we returned from Iran, so we happily flew to Denver to stay with Patty's parents. To our amazement, they graciously moved out of their home into an apartment so that we could have the full use of their home for our first year back in the States! We enrolled our children in a Christian School and settled into a normal routine. I was invited to speak to several churches around the country. The pressing issue that was always on our minds was, of course, what were we to do next? What do missionaries do who have been deported from the country they were serving in? Such a dilemma! In the early months of our time in Denver, I was approached by several ministries working with international students, who asked if I would be open to working with them. That might have been one direction in which I could have gone, but I had a powerful conviction that God had called me to the pastoral ministry. I continued to pray and wait to see how God would lead us. On one trip to California, I met some families and young people who were from the Evangelical Church of Iran. As I visited in their homes and met some who were in college, it occurred to me they might be open to having a pastor who was culturally sensitive to their needs and who could speak their language. Even though they were few in number, I had no way of knowing then how greatly they would increase in the years to come. I did not expect then how future Christians emigrating from Iran would feel rejected by the American church for its lack of vision for their pastoral needs. These believers found they did not fit into the American church. They were looking for a church experience similar to the one they had had in Iran: a family of faith, not merely a church program to attend. They longed for fellowship and friendship, yet many American churches did not meet these expectations. Others were shocked by the liberalism of the American Presbyterian Church. The Injili Church in Iran was, mostly, evangelical and Biblical in its beliefs. They adhered to the Westminster Confession of Faith, did not question the authority of the Bible, believed in trusting in Christ alone for salvation, and did not understand why the liberal church in America had turned Biblical faith into a political movement. The net result was that many who might have joined the ranks of the American church drifted away. Others were drawn to more conservative evangelical churches, often abandoning the Reformed faith they had been taught in Iran.

As I think back to my visit with those early immigrants from Iran and reflect on the waves of Iranians who have come to America, I cannot help but wonder how things might have been different if the American church had had a vision for shepherding them. On that first visit to California, I visited some large prominent Presbyterian churches and asked if they would be interested in having a person on staff who could reach out to the Persian Christians fleeing oppression in Iran. The answer I repeatedly received was, "We just do not have the budget for it." No one seemed interested in exploring ways to finance such a new ministry. Doors closed! How much of this reaction resulted from the political situation with the ongoing hostage crisis? God only knows. But it was a blow to my faith. Did the church now fear pursuing Kingdom of God goals because of some sort of nationalism? What had happened to being salt and light to our culture? I thought of all the believers I knew in Iran who every day faced the threat of a government who could haul them off to prison without a trial. They continued to pursue obedience to Christ by sharing their faith with Muslims. But why did my church in America not have the same vision to reach a group of people who were the fruit of years of missionary efforts in Iran and who were now living in their own communities? The result of all this is that today, while many American churches in California have Iranian members, many have dropped out of church completely.

I next made an appointment with the newly formed Samuel Zwemer Institute. I felt some hope, thinking certainly those who worked there would have some guidance for me. If my church was not interested in reaching out to Iranian believers and the many Muslims pouring into our country, certainly *they* would be. I was welcomed by the director and given the royal tour. It was impressive to think that there was such an organization that was dedicated to solid scholarship and passionate evangelism and discipleship of Muslim background believers, but it became very clear that resources would be difficult to find. I had no idea how I could utilize my experiences without some kind of financial support.

Sometimes we are faced with the fact that what seems logical to us is not the path God has chosen for us. The door to California was closed, but I turned my heart towards God and asked Him to lead us. He led us to the Washington, DC area of suburban Maryland.

CHAPTER TWELVE
THE BIRTH OF AN IRANIAN CHURCH

As all doors closed on my finding a ministry that would allow me to continue serving Iranians, God opened another door. The Church of the Atonement in Silver Spring, Maryland, had just begun their process of searching for a new pastor the summer that we returned from Iran. They had been given my name as a potential candidate and invited me to meet with the search committee. I later learned I was the first candidate they interviewed! Knowing little about them and still numb from our abrupt departure from Iran, I went into that interview feeling relaxed and non-committal. I was not sure how God was leading us, so I was not trying to secure the position. After going through months of poring over resumes, by God's grace they came back to me and called me to be their pastor!

Dr. William Miller was quite elderly at this time, but he occasionally wrote me encouraging letters. After we had been at Atonement for a few years, he wrote and introduced me to an Iranian Christian with whom he was in contact, a Mr. Saeed Mirbaha, asking me to reach out to him. I invited Mr. Mirbaha, a portly man with an infectious laugh, to one of our worship services. The day he visited our church, we invited him to have lunch with us after the service. It was a freezing February day. We enjoyed warm fellowship as he shared his testimony with us. He had become a believer in Jesus in Iran and shared how he went to see Bishop William Thompson, a beloved Bishop of the Anglican Church in Iran. Mirbaha had traveled a long distance hoping to be baptized, but Bishop Thompson wisely refused to baptize him without fully getting to know him first. But Mirbaha was not to be dissuaded so easily. He pointed out to the

Bishop that Philip baptized the Ethiopian eunuch without requiring him to undergo months of preparation. Apparently, his words were convincing enough that Mirbaha was truly converted to Christ, and the Bishop arranged for his baptism. At this point in his testimony, Mirbaha opened his Persian Bible and showed me Bishop Thompson's signature. Before he left that day, we prayed together, and what God laid on both of our hearts was that the Holy Spirit would lead us to other Iranians so that we might begin ministry together. Afterwards, Mirbaha smilingly said goodbye.

Sometime after, he called me to tell me that an Iranian woman had fled her abusive husband and had taken refuge in a church in our area. The church had helped her find a safe place to live; would I go visit her? I took my young daughter, Emily, with me since I did not feel it would be appropriate for me to visit her alone. She was living in a small apartment with no furniture; her newborn daughter was asleep on the floor wrapped in a small blanket. She greeted us warmly and we sat on the floor with her as she relayed her sad story. Her husband apparently had become enraged that she was pregnant and that she wanted to keep the baby; he had tried unsuccessfully to abort her baby by kicking her in the abdomen. As she spoke about how she had had to flee in terror, she seemed to relive the traumatic event all over again. I shared the Gospel with her, and she was eager to trust Jesus for her salvation and future. I relayed our conversation to Mr. Mirbaha, and we prayed together for her and thanked God that we now had our first new member of our church. Would there be others?

Tat and Patty in Front of the Church of the Atonement

We had little idea of how God was moving among the Iranians in our community. I have often been asked, how do you start a ministry among Iranians? As I look back on those early days, I realize how little I knew about ministering to them. Prayer played a major role. We did not know many Iranians, but we had told God that we were open to His leading. Again, we received a phone call from an Iranian. A young woman named Nushi was on the line. She told me how she had become a Christian and that she was perhaps the only Iranian Muslim who had ever converted to Christ! That is not an uncommon reaction since there had been so few Muslims who had converted to Christianity in the past. As I relayed to her about the church in Iran, and mentioned the Farsi Bible and hymn book, I sensed a great excitement in her voice and an eagerness to meet us. Nushi and her husband Mario later shared their testimonies with us. Mario, a Latino-American, had become a Christian, so Nushi decided she would become a more serious Muslim in response to his conversion. She went back to saying her daily prayers in Arabic and reading her Quran. But while her husband was away on a trip, she attended his church and listened to the message of the Bible out of curiosity about what he was hearing and believing. She told me it was not a dream or any other supernatural event that brought her to Christ. It just happened one morning that when she woke up, she had a deep conviction that what the Bible said was true and quietly committed her life to Christ. We now had our third member of our small church plant.

The next person the Lord brought into our budding fellowship was a gentleman named Saeed Roshdieh. He was an older man, married with three adult children, who introduced himself to me as a former teacher of the Quran. He had had a dream while visiting friends in Texas. A person bathed in a brilliant light visited him. He did not know who it was, but it set him on a path to learn more about God. Because he was a student of the Quran, he had been taught that there were certain verses in the Quran that, if memorized and repeated, would obligate Allah to answer your prayers. Mr. Roshdieh struggled with fierce anger; he knew it was a significant source of stress in his relationships with his family and friends. He determined to fast for two days, repeat the special verses of the Quran, and ask God to change his character. As he recalled, "I was not asking God for success or wealth, but just to change me." Two days passed, and he was filled with great optimism that he had been changed. The third day, he emerged from his room filled with the expectation and confidence that he was now a new man. He told me that some member of the family had knocked over a vase, shattering it. Before he knew it, he was yelling in anger. Suddenly, his heart sank, *not* because of a broken vase, but because he had not changed. He had put his faith to the test, and it had failed him.

He sank into a deep depression and wondered if he had been living a lie and misleading others to put their hope in a religion that was false.

Soon after this crushing realization, he drove towards the ocean. He fantasized about driving the car into the sea and ending his life. He felt defeated, depressed, and lost. The darkness of his depression was only magnified by the darkness of the night. He saw a sign for a motel and decided to spend the night and continue his plans for ending his life the next day. He checked into the motel and went to his room. Sitting there alone with his sorrows, with no one to console him, a little sign on the bedside table caught his eye: "Here is a gift for you." For a moment, he wondered who had known he would be here that night. Curiosity moved him, and he discovered the gift was a Bible. He opened it and found himself reading a story in the Gospels about Jesus healing a man possessed by an evil spirit. He was overwhelmed with amazement at what Jesus had done. *"That is my problem. I need to be delivered from evil."* He dropped to his knees and prayed to Jesus, "Jesus, if You could deliver that boy from evil, please deliver me from evil." The depression evaporated away, and to his amazement, he felt clean and whole. He felt so changed that he checked out of the motel and drove home. The next morning, he gathered his family around and made an announcement: "Jesus has changed me and to prove it, if any of you can make me angry, I will give you a hundred dollars." I can only imagine how his family felt. His son, with a smirk on this face, said, "Dad, get your checkbook ready for it won't be long before something makes you angry!" Miraculously, nothing upset Mr. Roshdieh for over a month! [13] Mr. Roshdieh then knew that the vision he had had years before was of Jesus.

The change that Christ brought about in Mr. Roshdieh's life had a great impact for Christ on his family. I had the honor of baptizing Effat, his beloved wife, who had also received Christ not long after. She lived a powerful life of witness until the day she left her earthly body. In the last years of her life, she had several Iranian caretakers. She insisted that SAT7-PARS satellite television was on all day, so each caretaker not only witnessed her life and heard her testimony, but were also subjected to many hours of Christian programming. Many of those Iranian caretakers came

---

13. After his month of victory over anger, he realized it had been only a short period of grace; he would now have to learn on a daily basis how to deal with any anger, God's way. Don't we all?

to faith in Christ. I had the privilege of visiting Effat in the last days of her life. Her face had a most beautiful radiance as we prayed together.

God continues to work mighty transformations in men and women through which He convinces others of the reality of Christ. Mr. Roshdieh became an elder in our church and was later ordained by his Baptist church to the Gospel ministry. He opened his home for weekly Bible studies for many years and served his Lord until the Lord took him home to Himself.

During the early days, we had many meetings in our own home as well. God brought many wonderful people into our life and it would require another book to tell all their stories! One of those who began coming to our home for Bible study was a lady whom Mr. Roshdieh had brought. She was a very kind, gracious lady. During these meetings, she surrendered her life to Christ. Soon afterwards, she asked me if she had to tell her husband about her conversion. He was a devout Muslim, and had just made a pilgrimage to Mecca on their way to America, just in case he never returned to the Middle East. This raised a challenging question for us. We concluded it was better that she not confront him yet, but to work on growing in Christ herself, witnessing to her faith by her attitude and actions, and praying about when she should tell him. After about six months, she agreed that the time had arrived.

She chose the day that she was going to tell her husband that she had become a follower of Jesus. We were all praying for her. She prepared his favorite meal, wore one of her nicest dresses, cleaned the house, and waited for him to arrive. After she greeted him warmly, they enjoyed the delightful meal she had prepared. She then mustered enough courage to say, "I have something very important to tell you. It may make you want to divorce me." I can only imagine the thoughts this poor man was having! *What could my wife have done that would lead me to consider divorce?* She certainly had his full attention now, so she continued, "I have been going to a Bible study and I have become a Christian." She braced herself for his reaction. To her utter disbelief, he laughed. This annoyed her, so she scolded him, "You are not taking me seriously! You are making fun of me!" "No! No!" He managed to say between laughs. "The reason I am laughing is that I am overjoyed! You see, I too have become a Christian!" He explained he had been worried about how he was going to tell *her!* He had recently enrolled in a Bible correspondence course and put his faith in Jesus too. Needless to say, the evening ended very well, with much rejoicing in the Lord. They were a key family in the founding of our church. Their son became a believer while in prison and I had the honor of baptizing him in the prison chapel on the Saturday evening before Easter in his mother tongue, Farsi.

It takes time to plant a church among immigrants from a Muslim background. We did not know many Americans who could help us. I was still the pastor of Church of the Atonement, so the time I could devote to this new ministry was limited. God brought us a helping hand in a young man named Larry Claremont who had some friendships with Iranians and joined us in the ministry. He faithfully served alongside us for many years. Eventually, we concluded we needed to meet in our church building rather than in homes. We held our first meeting in a classroom at Church of the Atonement in the afternoon. We had no music since no one had experience in leading worship in Farsi, but we did have a little homemade hymnbook; I remember the day Patty, on her keyboard, led us in singing our first song. This was before the Internet, so Patty had to teach our little congregation how to sing hymns. Culturally, Iranians sing solos rather than taking part in group singing. In the beginning, everyone sang at their own pace — and key — it sounded terrible. Patty had to teach them to follow her voice since they ignored the actual music. Gradually, Patty taught them more hymns and our little congregation grew in its delight in worshiping God. Later, we expanded to a roundtable discussion format where I spent most of the time answering questions and teaching the fundamentals of the Christian faith. Afterwards, we had a more formal time of worship in the chapel, followed by a time of fellowship with tea and Persian sweets. Our attendance during those early years averaged between fifteen to eighteen people.

Patty Leading Music at the Iranian Church in Silver Spring, MD

In the early 1990s, I felt God tugging at my heart to become even more involved in Persian ministry. I had from time to time been invited to speak at Iranian Christian International conferences. I could sense that God was doing a new thing among Iranians and I kept wondering if God was calling me to take part. There were several events that led me to believe that He wanted me to serve Him among Iranians. The first one came through hearing some statistics that shocked me: *There was only one trained Iranian Christian leader for every million Iranians.* I could count on my fingers the Iranian Christian leaders that I knew and wondered if God might be calling me to join them. Then I read that the vast majority of trained Christian leaders worked among those who spoke English. These facts troubled me more, for I knew two of the languages spoken by the people of Iran and I was not using them (Luke 12:48b). What excuse would I have to give to the Lord when I stood before him and He asked me what I had done with the talents He had given me? I realized there were many qualified pastors who could take my place in the English-speaking world. These factors led me to pray, seeking God's direction.

My ministry at the Church of the Atonement was fruitful, and I would have been happy staying there until I retired. I walked the two blocks to work every day, excited about the ministry God had given me. I was continuing to pray, however, for God to show me if He wanted me to minister to Iranians. One day, as I approached the door of the church, I sensed that my call to serve Christ at Atonement was lifted. It is hard to explain, but it felt as though I had been released, that somehow my heart wasn't in it the way it had been for over twelve years. I was perplexed at first, in a way not really sure how to deal with this new feeling. Wanting to test to see if it was actually from God, I decided to take some time to seek the counsel of some trusted Iranian leaders. I asked them to give me their honest opinions about my sense of being called to work with Persians. Over many months, every Iranian leader I talked to confirmed my call. Then I decided it was time to approach our mission board. I had served on the board of World Witness for over nine years. I had myself served as the chairman of the board and knew many of the members personally. However, World Witness did not have a current ministry to Iranians. I prepared to approach them about the possibility of their calling Patty and me to begin a ministry to Iranians, and wrote a position paper about how God was working in Iran and how I felt that Patty and I were uniquely qualified for such a ministry. I presented my paper and then waited to hear their reaction. They admitted that they had had no vision to work with

Iran but felt that since God had brought us to their denomination and they knew me well, they would extend a call to us to become full-time missionaries. They gave me the title *"Director of Persian Ministries,"* even though I had no one yet to direct. Not long after that, I informed the elders at the Church of the Atonement that Patty and I had been called by World Witness to be missionaries to the Persian-speaking world.

I was now free to devote all my time to the little fellowship of eighteen Muslim background believers who met at Church of the Atonement. During this time, we experienced a variety of reactions from our friends and co-workers. One very dear friend told me I had made a terrible decision. He called it professional suicide; I would fade from sight and no one would ever hear about me again! I thought back to our days in Carteret when we announced we were going to Iran and how negatively some reacted, and later how several Christians responded to us when we tried to find an organization who would hire us after we were deported from Iran. But armed with the conviction that this was what God was calling us to do, we obeyed. How glad I am that we did! We chose to listen to God, and He has blessed that decision more than we could have ever imagined.

With more time to do ministry, I began to lay the foundations for our becoming an official church. I knew that one of the greatest challenges I would face was that of addressing those attendees who wanted to be baptized solely for immigration purposes. The US government thankfully does not send immigrants back to a country where they might face persecution. It has long been established that if you are a Muslim and you convert to Christianity and want to practice it openly in Iran, you will most likely face persecution. This resulted in a constant flow of people visiting our church. Some immigration lawyers in the Washington, D.C. area were telling their clients to attend our church! I knew I needed a plan for how to witness to visitors while still being certain that those we were baptizing were genuine believers. The first policy we adopted as a church was that we would baptize no one until six months after they had prayed the sinner's prayer. The second policy was to let Iranian believers be the litmus test for our new converts. To facilitate this, I started weekly Bible studies in three different locations: Baltimore, Northern Virginia, and Silver Spring. I informed the church that I would be at each of these locations during the week and if they wanted to grow as Christians, they would be required to attend the one nearest their home. These meetings often ran very late into the night as we sang praises and worshiped God, studied His Word, and fellowshipped together. I knew that if this church was to survive, the believers had to be knit together as close friends. I knew how powerful friendships were in the Iranian culture and I believed many Iranian churches were failing because of the tendency for members to relate primarily to the pastor rather than each other. When pastors are made to be the central focus, unhealthy situations can develop. For instance, if the pastor hurts someone's feelings, the injured party usually stops attending church. However, if members maintain deep friendships within the church, offenses are less likely to result in estrangement. Therefore, it was good to see my congregation gathering in small groups. At the outset, I did most of the leading. As time passed, I invited others to lead the prayer time or host the meetings in their homes. This system gave us an opportunity to get to know those who wanted to be baptized and to answer their many questions. It also gave us time to test their sincerity and commitment, as I wanted to see them not only at Sunday worship but also to watch how they interacted with others in our midweek Bible studies.

One very key person during this stage of church planting was my dear brother Javad. Javad was a new believer, and we developed a deep bond. I had first learned of him when a Bible College student wrote me and told me he had given Javad a Farsi Bible and the student thought Javad was very open to the Gospel. I wrote Javad an official invitation to our Persian service and accompanied it with a map of our church's location. He came the very next Sunday. He was expecting to find a church full of Armenian Christians, and was shocked when I asked a brother named Mohammad (a Muslim name) to read the Scriptures that day. Javad was an outstanding student of the word and trusted Christ, and I had the honor of baptizing him. When we began the small group meetings, Javad went with me. We spent hours together discussing Bible passages and the needs of the church. He took copious notes of all my teachings. It was not long before I recognized a man of God who would be a good elder.

As our congregation grew, I knew we needed a leadership team; rather than calling them elders, we called our first leaders "servants" of the Lord. I decided we had to meet regularly and to make decisions together. After all, being of Presbyterian heritage, it seemed the right thing to do. I learned an important lesson in our first meeting in how to lead them in deciding as a group. We had one item on the agenda: *should we take up an offering or not?* It did not seem like a very controversial item to me, but I wanted us to decide together as a team. We prayed, I read some scripture about honoring one another, and I shared the item to be discussed. Three hours later, we had not yet come to a consensus! Not one of these dear believers could agree with any suggestion made by another person. Finally, in desperation, I announced, "Look! We will begin taking up an offering!" They all smiled and said that would be fine. What did this mean for the future? Was there any way to convince them to see the wisdom that others had? I now realized I was going to have to learn another way to show them how to function as leaders. I longed to have their input; after all, I was not an Iranian, and I wanted their cultural wisdom. The Lord led me to a new method of gleaning their wisdom without going through the painful exercise of discussing things and not being able to arrive at a consensus. Whenever we had major issues to be decided, I met individually with each member of the leadership team and heard their insights and suggestions. Then I presented a recommendation based on the input I had gathered from all of them. They then would most often vote for the proposal since they had all contributed to it, yet they did not lose face by having to accept views counter to theirs.

Iran is a shame-based culture.14 The roots of shame go back to the Garden of Eden, where Adam and Eve hid from God after disobeying Him out of shame. Shame is the feeling of loss of worth and goodness. In a shame/ honor culture, the most important factor in one's life is to protect one's honor, and the most dreaded experiences are those in which one is shamed. Honor is accumulated by one's family history, education, marriage, wealth, and title or position. Titles are very important and one must be diligent to call others by the correct title so as not to be disrespectful. The love language of honor is hospitality, thus an invitation to the homes of others is an important honor; having important guests coming to your home is equally important (consider Zacchaeus's response to Jesus' inviting Himself to his house in Luke 19:5). Honor is shown by standing up when others enter a room, greeting everyone. individually, flattering them, and giving them gifts. Dishonor is shown by pointing out failures in public, verbally attacking them, insulting their parents, mocking, and being sarcastic. The highest form of dishonor is to reject and avoid a person altogether. This extreme affront can lead the slighted party to take verbal revenge as gossip. I certainly did not want to insult any of our members by

---

14. Iran is constantly changing, and the emphasis on shame and honor is not as prevalent as it was in years past; however, it helps to understand the roots of the culture to which you are ministering.

causing them to lose face, which could have started a huge domino effect, eventually destroying our growing church family.

After forming the leadership team, the next step was to establish criteria for church membership. We had been using a statement of faith with all those being baptized, so we already considered them members of the Body. However, we felt it necessary to have a mechanism by which we all could make a covenant of membership together. I preached for several weeks about what it meant to be a responsible member of the church of Christ. We then set a date on which each baptized believer would state his or her commitment to Christ and specifically to our church. We had prepared a statement of faith that we all read together; each person was to come forward to sign their name and date in a leather-bound book, which would serve as the official record of our church's membership. Approximately 45 individuals signed the commitment notebook. It was a landmark day for the Iranian Christian Church of Washington, D.C.

In the year that followed, I taught a great deal about the character qualities that godly leaders must have and the particular functions they are to perform in the Body of Christ. Then I addressed how elders should be chosen by the body. I realized that in the New Testament, Paul often appointed elders in new churches; I considered that option. But because our church had grown to over fifty members, I wanted the Holy Spirit to lead us to those elders that He was calling. And now that we had official membership, our elders would be chosen from our membership; we believed God would lead us to do that as a church. This solved the problem of people nominating those who were active in the church but had not been willing to sign the membership covenant. I had taught for many weeks on the Biblical qualifications for elders leading up to the day we would begin the election process.

The Sunday before the election of elders, I explained the process to the congregation. We would not be using the typical election method in which the congregation chose between slates of candidates; I believed it would not work in an honor/shame culture. Those not elected would feel shamed, possibly causing them to leave the church. I believe the Lord guided me to another method. We were a small congregation and having three elders would serve us best. My leadership team agreed. I asked the congregation to spend the next week praying for the leading of the Holy

Spirit in choosing our new elders. They would be given the opportunity to nominate three individuals from the membership, but they could not nominate themselves. The three with the most votes would be those whom the Holy Spirit had chosen. The following Sunday, we worshiped, and then began the election process. Each member was given a numbered slip of paper and told to write the names of the three people they believed God wanted to lead our congregation. They did not have to sign their name, but we knew the total number of ballots we had distributed. As the four members of the leadership team tallied the votes, there was a sobering sense of the presence of the Lord as we waited to hear the results. There were three men who received most of the votes. I was relieved because there was no doubt about who were to be our elders. The Holy Spirit had spoken. The congregation stood and clapped and we praised God together.

Despite all our efforts, not everyone was glad with the results. One particular brother was certain God had chosen him to be a leader in our congregation and in anger he stood outside the church telling members that the election was Satanic because he was not chosen. I was relieved that he was not chosen. Through the months that he had been attending our church, his method of leadership was to do things for our people to make them feel indebted to him. He used spiritual flattery to gain a foothold in the hearts of others. He offered to come to people's homes and pray for them and his actions swayed many. I had to fight the urge to block him from becoming an elder. It was a good thing that I had let the Holy Spirit set him aside; he could not blame me for the result, but had to face the decision of the entire church. It was a powerful lesson for the church. Allow Christ to build His church! He does a far better job than we can do!

I want now to address the spiritual battles that take place when sharing Christ with Muslims and seeking to plant a church. It is beyond the scope of this book to reveal all the ways the enemy came against us during our ministry in Washington. But I believe it is important for me to emphasize that planting this church was not without great attacks from the enemy. The first battleground was in constant attacks on the Word of God. Topics such as the sinful nature of man, the wrath of God, the Trinity, and forgiving others were just a few that were continually disputed. The enemy often worked through different people in our congregation. I preached one Sunday on the nature of sin and the elder assisting me in worship came to the pulpit afterwards and thanked me for a wonderful sermon; he then told the congregation that when I had said all have sinned, I had not been talking about *them*. Another man hated the Old Testament and did not approve of our reading a Psalm each Sunday. One Sunday he stood up just before I was to preach and with a loud voice announced that they should not listen to my preaching, since I was trying to make Jews out of them all! It was some time before we restored order. Another brother invited me to his home for lunch and after a delightful meal, he took out a piece of paper and read me twenty-seven sins that I had committed! For example, when I prayed, I dishonored God by putting my hands in my pocket. I listened to the entire list without comment. I knew he was an angry man, and arguing or defending myself would have been pointless.[15]

    Another tool the enemy used was in creating conflicts between us. In a shame culture, any kind of perceived disrespect causes disgrace and hurt. As an American, I was not even aware of some ways my actions hurt my Iranian brothers and sisters, and I suppose they were not always aware of how they hurt me. I observed that when Iranians come to Christ and become a part of the Body of Christ, they are usually ecstatic. They loved the close fellowship and going to each other's homes. But it is here that culture collides with Kingdom of God principles. They are not prepared for the fact that everyone in the church does not follow the Iranian cultural rules of friendship. For instance, if we are all one big family, why did one family not invite my family to their child's birthday party? That was perceived as disrespectful, and many conflicts arose. My Iranian counselors advised me it would be better for me not to have much social interaction with the members of my church. If someone specifically invited me to their home, I did go, but Patty and I did not fall into the trap of socializing with only a few select families. Other situations that caused conflict were when two single men decided to minimize expenses by sharing an apartment. After watching how quickly a friendship might deteriorate into a major conflict, we enacted a church policy, in which we met with the two parties and wrote a contract outlining who was responsible for paying the rent and utilities and how household chores were to be shared, among other details. They signed it and the church kept a copy. This worked very well in most cases. Another major source of conflict was in handling money. New immigrants often needed money, so they would single out the members who were more established and ask to borrow money. This often kept more mature and well-established Iranians from wanting to be active in Iranian churches. If they lent money to needy fellow members, those

---

15. A few years ago, this same man called me from California and apologized for his disruptive behavior. He had grown spiritually during the intervening years.

members felt indebted to them. When they couldn't pay back the loan, they often stopped coming to church, ashamed to face the person to whom they owed money. The lender would also become irritated and angry since the loan had not been repaid. We had to come up with a solution. We wanted to help our members who were in financial distress. After long discussions with the elders, we informed the church that they were not to borrow money from each other; rather, they were to inform the elders about their financial needs. We told them the church was not a lending bank; however, we would give them financial help after assessing their needs. If anyone wanted to help another member, they could give the funds to the church and designate the name of whom they wanted to help, but the person would be told the help was from the church. The person receiving the help would be informed that this was a onetime gift from the church and they did not owe the church anything. However, when they were financially able, they were encouraged to give a gift to the church to help others who might be in need.

There were many other instances of cultural challenges in our new flock, but in every case where the enemy sought to create division, the Holy Spirit provided us with insights and resources to preserve the peace and unity of the church.

CHAPTER THIRTEEN
THE DIASPORA

Today, Iranians can be found in almost every time zone around the world, but this was not always the case. The first wave of Iranians left Iran in the 1950s and 1960s mainly to pursue academic goals. The intellectuals of Iran favored the educational system of France, which had a significant influence on the educational system in Iran. Others turned to America in pursuit of practical higher education. They wanted degrees in medicine, engineering, and technology, hoping to return to Iran to use their skills to advance their country. Later, Iranians came to learn more about the oil industry and many prospective students moved to Texas. As Iran's income from oil mushroomed, the Shah sent many Iranians to America to be trained by the US Air Force. This was the first wave of Iranians moving to the west, thus initiating the modern Iranian Diaspora.

The second wave of mass immigration occurred in the months that led up to the Islamic Revolution and during the year that followed. I am uncertain whether there is any accurate way to report the numbers of Iranians who fled Iran. Obviously, those who were associated with the Shah's government made up a large number of them, but there were others who left as well. Many had become accustomed to a western way of life and had the means to leave. Minorities like Armenians and Assyrians left in droves. Today, I am told that 75% of Assyrians have migrated to the USA and Australia. Likewise, 50% of Armenians have also left. In the early years of the Revolution, Protestant Christians also emigrated. Bishop Dehghani and his family left after their son Bahram was murdered. Because I was living in Tehran during the first year after the Islamic

Revolution (1979-80), I witnessed almost weekly the departure of believers from the Evangelical Church of Iran and the persecution that was becoming more and more pervasive.

The third wave of immigration was more prolonged. In many ways, it continues. There are many reasons for Iranians continuing to abandon their homeland. Some are weary from the hardships of life in modern Iran. Others experienced financial difficulties and fled to Turkey to begin new lives. Others were being persecuted by the Regime and had to flee, many because of their Christian faith. Initially, most of them went to Turkey, where they could register as refugees with the United Nations and possibly immigrate to the West.

The great Iranian Diaspora had an extensive effect on how we ministered to Iranians. No longer was ministry confined to a geographical location within the borders of Iran, since thousands of Iranians no longer lived in Iran. The mission field had shifted, but so had the Iranian Church; as Iranian Christians emigrated, countries like Germany, England, and the US became new centers of Persian ministry. Church leaders who had left Iran were now leading fellowships in exile. Concurrently, Muslims were coming to Christ outside of Iran and were leading small fellowships. I met a brother in Norway who was active in a Norwegian Lutheran church, yet was also pastoring a small group of Iranians who had come to Christ. I spent several days walking the streets of Oslo with him and learning about his spiritual journey. He shared that he had been imprisoned in Iran for his political activities. Apparently, he had been a part of a group actively undermining the regime. He may have been unjustly charged with trumped-up anti-government activities. It is a common practice in Iran to dispose of undesirable people by falsely accusing them of treasonous activities. While in prison, he met an American inmate who was imprisoned on drug dealing charges. This American had attended Sunday school in his youth and was a wonderful source of Bible stories. To pass the time, my friend prodded the American man for information about Christianity. He later escaped to Norway and lived in a refugee camp. A local Norwegian church invited refugees to attend its church; my friend quickly accepted the invitation, wanting to hear more of the Bible stories he had heard in prison. While he was entering the church building through a back door, he passed the kitchen and saw an older man washing coffee cups. He asked a bystander, "Who is that man?" The answer changed his life: "He is our pastor." At that moment, he thought to himself, *I want to know that man's God.*

The other change that became clear was that the believers in the Diaspora began to awaken to the idea that they could now minister to others in the Diaspora as well as to those inside the country. Not only had the mission field shifted, but a new type of missionary movement was also occurring. Whereas in Iran, witnessing to others had become riskier, this was not the case outside Iran. In fact, there seemed to be a holy boldness that was prompting Iranians to share Christ with their family and friends. During one of my trips to Switzerland, I met a family who had all converted to Christ. What was astounding to me was that they had never met another Iranian Christian! They had not seen a Farsi Bible, never heard a Farsi praise song. They had learned all they knew about Christ via telephone contact with an Iranian in Canada who befriended them and shared the Gospel with them. What a joy it was for them to know they weren't alone in their faith and to hear hymns and teachings in their own language!

Technology, such as satellite television and the Internet, was eventually introduced to the world after the Diaspora and played an even greater role in fulfilling the Great Commission. The first Farsi Christian website that was developed was Farsinet.com. It was a blend of business ads, Christian sermons, and a plan to read through the Bible in a year. One very helpful aspect was the directory of worldwide Persian Churches. Today, there is a multitude of Iranian Christian websites.

I believe that my involvement with SAT-7 PARS was one of the most rewarding aspects of my ministry. SAT-7 PARS is a Farsi language 24/7 Christian satellite ministry. It follows the ethos of the SAT-7 family of channels, which is to provide Biblically sound Christian programming presented by Farsi speakers for the Farsi speaking world. The concept is that when Iranians in Tehran tune in to the channel they see Persians speaking about how the Christian faith has answers for their unique life's challenges; thus, they can see that Christianity is not some western ideology invading their world, but a universal truth that applies to them as well. Another distinction is that they teach the core teachings of Christianity while avoiding controversial denominational preferences. When controversial topics are presented, the teacher can explain how dedicated Christians approach them differently. The teacher then gives reasons for these differences, thus maintaining a sense of respect for other Christian traditions. What I love about SAT-7 PARS is that it controls all of its programming; unlike other Christian satellite ministries that sell time to individual ministries, it maintains a consistency in its teaching in its programming. I was invited to be a part of the steering committee that set the groundwork for what would become the channel today. We began by airing a few hours a week on the Arabic SAT-7 channel. The very able Sara Afshari, who had studied theology in the UK and was a missionary with the Anglican Church, led us. The board meeting where we chose the name for our channel took place in Dubai; we were staying at the Korean guest house. Rev. Marc Edgar, who served faithfully with me for many years, suggested the name SAT-7 PARS. There was little debate, and the name was adopted.

Early on, I was asked to serve as chairman of the board, a great honor for me. But what has brought me the greatest joy has been the times they asked me to teach on air. They asked me to lead a program on Christian Discipleship, called DOTA (Discipleship on the Air — DOTA.net). This course was initially developed for ministering to the house church movement in China. It was the answer to the question of how to help a house church movement grow and stay on target when there are no trained teachers? DOTA used a Bible-centered method, which taught a group how to study together. They asked me to demonstrate this method with six Iranians, so that those in Iran might not only read about this method but see it in action. My ninety hours of teaching were recorded and have been aired multiple times on air. It is one of the most effective tools for doing discipleship I have ever seen. Later, I was asked to teach a thirteen-episode program on Christian Marriage for SAT-7 PARS. To assist me in this, I invited an Iranian couple I had married years before to accompany me to Finland where we recorded it. What a powerful time it was as I taught the Biblical principles of marriage, along with the testimony and insight of this couple!

I am sure there will be many more technological advancements made in the future, so it will be exciting to see how God uses them to reach more and more people for the gospel!

Because Iran was closed to us for any kind of personal ministry, I felt God was leading me to investigate the possibilities of taking Iranian believers on mission trips to Turkey. Few seemed to be focused much on Turkey, even though there was a growing Iranian population there. Rev. Corley was living in Istanbul while shepherding the little Iranian flock that met in the old Armenian Church near the big bazaar. Mr. Corley had asked me to come to Istanbul for two weeks so that he could take some vacation time; I was to live in his apartment while preaching and leading prayer meetings in his stead. I accepted, but decided to take a mature Iranian believer with me. The Iranian Church in San Jose introduced me to Brother Fareed, who agreed to go with me; we met up in Istanbul. We immediately became good friends. Apparently, there were two American students who had been there for a few weeks living in a small hotel, praying and making friends with the Iranian guests, so we decided to visit them. The hotel was small and crowded with one toilet per floor. Most of the guests were Iranian, and it was quite obvious that they were financially limited. However, they seemed very open to hearing the gospel. Most days, I sat in the lobby as people lined up to meet with me and share their stories. They listened attentively to my presentation of the gospel. During that two-week trip, Brother Fareed and I spent most of our time with the hotel residents.

As we became closer to this group, we often shared meals with them. We contributed some money, and they cooked and invited us to share it with them. On one such evening in particular, as I entered the common area where we gathered for dinner, I noticed a man sitting in a fetal position in the corner of the room. I was rather distressed at the sight and asked the others who he was. "Oh, he is Mohsen! He has been depressed for days." As others were talking together and laughing, I could not take my eyes off him. Finally, not being able to stand it any longer, I went and sat down next to him. "Mohsen, I do not know what horrible things have happened to you but this is what I do know: if you call on the name of Jesus Christ, He can help you." There was absolutely no response from Mohsen. That night, I prayed for him and wondered what I could do to help him out of his deep depression. The next morning at ten, Brother Fareed and I returned to the hotel. As we walked into the lobby, Mohsen ran up to me. He had taken a shower, put on nice clothes, and had a big smile on his face. As he saw me, he blurted out, "I was dead, but now I am alive!" I was stunned! "What happened?" I inquired. "Well, I began thinking last night. If a big American man can come to my room all the way from America, sit next to me and talk to me in my mother tongue, there must be a God who cares! So I asked Jesus to help me and He did." Once again, God had allowed me to be a witness to the faithfulness of His Word and to witness its power to revive one who had been dead in his sin and give him new life. I felt that day that if Mohsen had been the only one to believe in the Lord Jesus, the trip would have been a major success.

The following year, I returned to Istanbul with a larger team, so most of the team had to stay in a hotel. As one of my team members was checking in, he met an Iranian man, shared the gospel with him, and the man prayed to receive Christ! This certainly was a great beginning and encouragement for all of us. As we surveyed the situation, we prayed asking God for guidance. One brother reported that there were long lines of Iranians at the American consulate and that there were other Iranians charging them $10 to fill out the forms they needed to submit to the consulate to get an appointment. He suggested we assist our fellow Iranians for free. We noticed that a hotel across from the Consulate had a nice teashop. Our plan was to assist the Iranians in filling out their forms without charging them; we then invited them to be our guests in the tearoom where several team members were waiting to share the gospel with them. The plan worked beautifully. Before we knew it, we had a room full of people sitting around tables with grateful hearts, listening to testimonies and hearing the gospel. God used this ministry, and we saw many come to faith in Christ. Now we had a new challenge: where could we gather to disciple these new brothers and sisters? We were not far from the Dutch Chapel where the International Church met, so I made an appointment with the pastor and asked if we could have a room in the church to disciple our new converts. He graciously gave his permission. Thus, the third step in our outreach was accomplished. One of our team members, a pastor who had the gift of teaching, set up discipleship training in one of the classrooms in the Dutch Chapel. We provided refreshments and lunch for those who came. This mission trip resulted in more than thirty Iranians coming to faith, doubling the membership of the local Persian Church. As a group, we believed God had blessed our time and had faithfully given us spiritual fruit.

As team leader, I learned a few lessons worth sharing. The first year, I had only one team member, but this time I had five. I had not met some of our team members beforehand, which turned out to be a mistake. I had tried giving some guidelines for our team ministry, but I did not expect some ways my team members would respond to the needs they saw among the immigrant Iranians. Apparently, our team stood out as visiting Iranian Americans. In fact, some on our Iranian team could not speak Farsi without using English words. A few times an Iranian from Istanbul who was talking to a team member looked at me, asking me what he was saying! The biggest problem, however, was that we were perceived as those who had money, so our team was accosted by many sob stories. The result was that one team member began giving out $20 bills to individuals and, as you may have guessed, he soon had a large crowd following him! When he brought this crowd to the Persian church, the local leaders pulled me aside and confronted me with this. They said, "Your team is making the church just like a mosque!" Those were hard words to hear, so we had to make a new rule: **Do not give money to anyone. You may buy someone food if they are hungry, but do not give them money!**

The climax of this trip came when we planned to show the "Jesus" film at the church. We were going to invite all our contacts to the film, followed by a light supper. I was worried that having so many people together might cause a conflict. I also worried that we might have technical difficulties since in the past something always went wrong during these types of events. I was acutely aware of the spiritual battle we were in. A few days before, I had been returning to the Corley's apartment where I was staying; as I reached the top step, an invisible arm knocked me down the flight of stairs. Other than some bruises and a broken watch, I was relatively unharmed, but it awakened in me a new realization of the spiritual battle we were fighting. I asked one brother who lived in Istanbul if we could use his small one-room flat as an upper room to pray for the outreach we had planned that evening. Several of us spent much of that day praying. When the time came for the program to begin, we had nearly sixty men, women, and children crammed into the sanctuary of the Armenian Church. One of our team welcomed everyone and explained the evening program. The lights were switched off and the projector's light flashed on the screen. The crowd settled down and for the duration of the film, were completely silent. When it was over, one of the pastors who was with me addressed the group. He presented the gospel and reviewed what they had just seen. He then gave an invitation for them to pray the sinner's prayer with him. After the prayer, he asked all those who prayed to receive Christ to stand. To the amazement of all, every single person stood. We all broke into applause for Jesus!

These mission trips had a significant effect on me. I sensed that the Holy Spirit was working among Iranians in a much different way than He had in the time Patty's and my parents had served in Iran. It seemed that a window of heaven over the people of Iran had been opened and God had become much more transcendent than previously. I also realized that I had so much more to learn about how to minister effectively among Iranians. I wanted to learn from Iranian pastors how to live and witness among Iranians, and how to explain Biblical truths more effectively so Iranians could understand better. Much of the methodology that I have used during my ministry has been gained at the feet of trusted Godly men. I learned from listening to their witnessing to others how important it was to **use culturally relevant stories and illustrations.** I was sitting in a hotel room in Istanbul listening to a team member discuss why the Incarnation was necessary. He asked the young man, "If your father knew you were in trouble here in Turkey, what would he do? He would call his friends here in Istanbul to come and visit you. If you needed money, he would make sure someone helped you. But let's say after sending his friends your problems were not solved. What would a good father do? He would get on a plane and come visit you himself! That is exactly what God did. He sent his prophets but they could not fix us, so he put on humanity and came to visit us. He is the only one who can fix you." As this parable was being presented, I saw a light go on in the mind and face of the listener as he began to understand the gospel.

Through the years, I have heard hundreds of testimonies about how Iranians have come to faith in Christ. I have thought much about the many ways in which God has revealed Himself to Iranians. There is one common thread that runs through most of them: each had a dream of Jesus. Before I share some of these amazing dreams, let me say a word to my brothers and sisters who do not believe God uses dreams today to reveal Himself. I had always been leary of dreams as well, and for most of my life saw little spiritual benefit in them. However, I have changed my mind after listening to myriads of Iranians testify about the role a dream had played in their hearing God's call to faith in Christ.

One scenario involves those who had begun reading the Bible but were uncertain whether it was the truth. After all, for most of their lives, they had been taught that the Quran was the latest revelation of God and that the New Testament had been tampered with, thus making it untrustworthy. What was most interesting was that the dream of Jesus occurred after they had read the Bible and served to verify to them that it was God's Word. And to make this even more compelling, the dream would many times consist of Jesus quoting a verse that they had read accompanied by a personal invitation to follow Him. The dream personalized Jesus for them. Muslims are discouraged from thinking they can have a personal relationship with God, so when a dream follows their reading the Bible it touches them deeply as they discover God is a Person who is reaching out to them. Thus, it is important to put the Word of God into the hands of our Muslim friends.

The other scenario is a dream that prompted the person to seek a New Testament to find out more about Jesus. A woman in Mashhad told me, "I was deeply depressed and hopeless because my husband had divorced me. During that time, I visited the home of a friend and noticed a black book on the coffee table; it seemed to call out to me. I asked my host about the book. She told me it was the Bible. I asked if I could read it and she loaned it to me for one day. I took the book home and had not been reading more than five minutes when an overwhelming desire to meet the author overcame me." That very night, she had a dream. In the dream, she saw herself with her head on the lap of a man in a brilliant white robe. His hand was touching her head and as he gently stroked her hair, all her anger, bitterness and despair drained out of her heart. I learned later that she had given her heart to Jesus and had started a house church in her home!

The most dramatic dream I ever heard was from a brother I met in Denmark. I was visiting an Iranian Christian's home Bible study. One of the men who attended seemed to have a special glow about him. Maybe not quite as dramatic as the glow Moses had when he came down from the presence of God, but he definitely stood out. He sat next to me and introduced himself. I asked him the question I have asked hundreds of Iranians, "How was it that God revealed to you that Jesus is the Son of God?" I never tire of hearing these stories. He told me his story. He had left Iran because he could not tolerate living under the restrictions of Islam, and chose to live in Denmark because he had heard that Denmark was a secular society so he would not have to deal with religious people. Therefore, he was shocked to learn that most of his co-workers were Christians! This distressed him but he found them to be very pleasant, so he tolerated their religious conversations… until they started witnessing to him. In self-defense, he decided to test their faith; he intended to prove to them they were wasting their time and his. One night as he sat on the edge of his bed, he prayed for the first time in his life. "Jesus, let's get this straight. I do not believe in you, but if you do exist, it is up to You to show me." He drifted off to sleep in full confidence that nothing would happen, and that he could report back to his co-workers that their faith was in vain.

That night, he dreamed that he was suspended in the air face to face with Jesus on the cross. Visibly moved by what he had dreamed, he said, "I could see the crown of thorns on Jesus' head and the beads of blood on his face. But what was most shocking were his eyes! They were like laser beams, seeing right into my heart. Then He spoke, 'I did this for you!' At these words, my entire body began trembling, and I was drenched in perspiration. I fell out of bed and lay there on the floor, facedown; all I could say was, 'I surrender!' That is how I came to faith in Jesus."

There were many more mission trips and many more wonderful dreams, but there is not room in one book to record them all. However, I would like to describe a very special mission trip that I took with my father and my brother, Bill. It was in the mid-1990s — we decided to go to Baku, Azerbaijan with an Iranian Christian who was an Azeri whose family originated in the city of Ganja. We arrived on Turkish Airways, which allowed us to have an overnight stay in Istanbul before we arrived in Baku. Azerbaijan was still emerging from the grip of seventy years under the iron hand of Stalin-era control. Its poverty was evident everywhere. We had been offered to rent an apartment — sight unseen — that belonged to an officer in the Azerbaijan army who was so poor he took his family to his village and rented his apartment to us for $100 a week. We climbed the stairs of a building that appeared to have survived a direct bomb attack. Finally, after climbing several flights of stairs, we arrived at the door of our apartment. The door was iron plated, and we had five different keys to unlock it. As we ventured in, we found dusty rooms with broken furniture. There was one bedroom with two beds and a kitchen with a few pots and plates. The greatest disappointment was that there was no water! We did our best to settle in and get some rest. The next morning, we had water, but it was bright orange. Because my father was a veteran of third-world challenges, he filled the tub with water and the minerals and dirt settled. We then boiled it to use for cooking. Bill discovered a bread shop nearby, so he bought us a fresh loaf of Russian bread. One piece of that bread staved off hunger for most of a day. We joked it must have had sawdust in it! The first day, we went shopping for food. We soon discovered there were no restaurants open due to the economic crisis. We also noticed that average people wore the same clothes every day. We learned how to take the local buses to go into town, where we spent most of the day talking to people and handing out gospel tracts.

One day, we ventured to another part of Baku and found ourselves in the middle of a large plaza. We had approximately one hundred gospel tracts left, so we wanted to be wise in how we distributed them. As I wondered how we should best use our limited resources, I felt the Lord saying to stay in the middle of the square and simply pray for a while. I prayed that the Holy Spirit would bring the people to us in whose hearts He had been working. So we stood in that spot; gradually, people began moving towards us. As they approached us, I said in Azeri, "We have a message for you from God, who loves you." They took the tract respectfully and asked, "Can we keep it?" "O yes, it is a gift for you." God brought many to us that day and we had the distinct sense that these were divine appointments.

I learned a lesson that day that has affected my approach to sharing the Good News with Muslims. **Ask God to lead you to those in whom God is already at work.** I became far more effective in ministering to those whose hearts had already been prepared than by merely scattering seeds far and wide. This meant that prayer became very vital as I sought discernment about whom I should witness to. In a shame-based culture, it is easier to witness to those who are already seeking, as they feel more in control of the discussion and the questions being asked.

On that same trip, I visited the Iranian Islamic Center's reading room as there was a strong emphasis from the Azeris of Iran to promote Islam in Azerbaijan. As I was perusing the Islamic literature, which I could not read, a friendly cleric greeted me in Farsi. He asked me why I was in Baku. I told him I was a teacher of the "Ingil" (English Bible) which seemed to impress him. He asked if he could show me something that had been passed down to him by his father. He disappeared for a minute, then returned with a Farsi Bible. His father had asked that he never dispose of this book. Opening the fly page, he showed me, to my amazement, that Dr. William M. Miller had signed it. Apparently, this man's father had been a friend of Dr. Miller, who had given him this Bible as a gift. He continued to tell me he was reading it. Amazingly, I was standing in the middle of an Islamic reading room in Baku, talking to a cleric who was reading the Word of God that had been given to his father by a Presbyterian missionary! I had to smile and look up to heaven and praise God. But it was also yet another experience that reminded me how very important it was to get the Word of God in Persian to Persian speakers.

I love to hear how God has used the Bible to bring Iranians to faith. There was a brother in our church who told me that his sister worked in a bank in Iran; she and her staff were very fearful of the future. He asked me to help him find verses about peace in the Bible. I compiled five or six verses and gave them to him. He included these verses in his next letter to his sister without giving the references. Two weeks later, he received a letter from his sister. "I did not know you were so poetic, dear brother! Your words have brought such peace to me. I took your letter and read it to our staff at the bank and they have all asked for copies and want you to write more." My friend admitted to his sister that those were verses from the Bible and he urged her to get a copy of the Ingil. I wonder whether those bank tellers came to faith in Jesus. "Faith comes from hearing, and hearing the words of Christ." (Romans 10:17)

On a mission trip to Sweden, where I taught annual conferences for several years, I saw much fruit from teaching God's Word. The small church would fill up with Iranian and Afghan refugees; the Iranians sat in the front and the Afghans, from the Hazaras people, sat in the back. The Hazaras people, who lived mainly in the mountainous area of central Afghanistan, were of Mongolian and Central Asian descent and descendants of Genghis Khan who invaded Afghanistan in the 13th Century. They had often been the victims of ethnic cleansing, slavery, and looting mostly at the hands of the Taliban. The Hazaras who were at my conference had all lived in Iran, where they were day laborers. Due to their Mongolian appearance, they were harassed in Iran and abused as well. When they came to an Iranian church in Sweden, they were naturally on guard. Many of them had been day laborers in Iran, so they understood my Farsi very well. For most of the conference, they sat stiffly and unemotionally, listening to my teachings on the blessings of knowing Christ. When we read the section about the blessings of being able to forgive our enemies, I sensed their increasing tension. It was not an easy subject for men who had been deeply hurt by their experiences in Iran. However, something very unexpected happened. One of the Iranian ladies stood up and asked permission to speak. She turned to the Afghan constituency and spoke to them.

She said, "I know you have suffered at the hands of my countrymen in Iran. You were treated unjustly; some of you never got paid. And I know for you to sit here with us Iranians has not been easy. But God has put it in my heart to ask for your forgiveness on behalf of the people of Iran. We have hurt you; will you forgive us?"

There was an awkward moment as we all held our breath. We could hear the sound of gentle sobs in the audience. And then one by one, the Afghan brothers forgave their Iranian brothers and sisters. At that moment, I was convinced the main purpose of my coming to Sweden was for this one experience. On that day, the entire spirit of our conference changed. The Afghan brothers asked me to have dinner with them that night, which I did, and we laughed together as I shared with them my travels in their country and they relayed how difficult it had been to leave their families in Iran or Afghanistan and the challenges of being known as Christian among other Afghans. It was such a sweet time of building each other up in encouragement and support. "Behold, how good and pleasant it is when brothers dwell in unity." (Psalm 133:1)

At this same conference, I met a Kurdish lady who showed me all the scars on her arms from the cigarette burns she had endured while being tortured by the Islamic Regime in Iran. She had been a Kurdish nationalist who had been imprisoned for her resistance to the central government. The Kurds are Sunnis and were greatly persecuted at the beginning of the Revolution; many were imprisoned. She was a tough-looking lady and stood out among the other attendees. I asked her, "Are you a believer in Jesus?" "Oh yes," she replied enthusiastically. "Well, then, how did you meet Jesus?" She smiled as if to say, *I thought you would never ask.* "While I was in prison, we had one hour a day in the yard to get some fresh air. On one particular day, the guards returned me to the wrong cell, which happens once in a while. As I sat in the cell, I noticed a strange book on the table. I picked it up and saw the title, The Holy Bible, so because I had nothing better to do, I began reading. I began with the Gospel of Matthew, but when I got to chapter 5, I read the first few verses and then put it down. Later I was returned to my cell and fell asleep that night not thinking much of what I had read. That night I was awakened by the presence of a man in shining white robes standing in the corner of my cell, inviting me to follow him. I told Him, 'I do not follow anyone!' and went back to sleep. This happened for six nights in a row. Each night I told the man in the white robes, 'I follow no one.' The seventh night, the vision changed; I saw Jesus sitting down on a hilltop and multitudes of people coming up the hill to sit at His feet. I remembered what I had read about Jesus in the Ingil and, in my vision, I do not know how it happened, but I got up from bed and followed the others up the hill and sat at his feet. The next morning, I felt as though I was a new person. My hate was gone, and I knew Jesus was my Savior."

In all my travels throughout the Diaspora, it became more and more evident that I was witnessing a wonderful time of God's visitation among the Iranian people. My heart was deeply encouraged, and I was increasingly motivated to continue teaching and ministering to the Persian-language church.

NO STRANGER

CHAPTER FOURTEEN
THE EXPLOSIVE GROWTH OF CHRISTIANITY

There can now be no doubt that Iran is one of the most fruitful places on earth for the gospel. Many who are much more informed than I have written about this amazing phenomenon. For others like me, who had spent years in Iran before this spiritual tsunami awakened the hearts of many to follow Christ, it seems like a miracle. My parents and those who labored for years in Iran for the past two hundred years most likely never dreamed of such a day. However, in God's gracious providence, every faithful witness of past generations was part of God's overall plan for the nation of Iran. A host of other factors came into play; political, social, and cultural factors, and many more of which we are not even aware. I am sure missiologists will study this deep and widespread awakening in Iran for years to come.

I hope it has become clear that Patty and I have had our lives deeply affected by the people and culture of Iran. We have spent the better part of our lives involved with Iranians who have converted to Christianity. We have provided pastoral leadership to two church plants in North America. Patty served as a music worship leader and I as a pastor. We have remained in constant contact with the Iranian church and its leadership throughout the Diaspora and with those still inside the country. So what I am about to say is not an academic or scientific analysis of what has been taking place in Iran. Others have done that much more ably than I could. Rather, I want to give you my observations as a second-generation missionary who has had the honor to labor alongside Iranian leaders and hear firsthand the stories of God's gracious work among their people. I believe this is an important distinction I need to make as I share with you my personal observations of what are the factors that have driven this glorious great awakening in Iran.

A Nation Thirsty For God

In all great Awakenings, there are varying historical and sociological factors. God moves by bringing many loose threads together and weaving them into spiritual movements. Humanistic movements, by comparison, eventually topple and collapse. Every ideology raised up against the knowledge of God will eventually falter and fail. In the Soviet Union, communism crumbled because it was not a sustainable system. I visited Azerbaijan in 1994, just after it had declared its independence, and was shocked at the poverty that had engulfed that nation. In Iran today, we are witnessing a nation that is bankrupt. The false beliefs of Islam are bearing fruit — *rotten* fruit. Every ideology that is raised up against the authority of God is doomed to fail. I have seen this in the personal lives of friends and family. The certain demise of worldly belief structures should help us in understanding the events in Iran and Afghanistan, and should also be a warning to us about much of Western culture.

On the contrary, God's truth brings life. Matthew, quoting Isaiah, spoke of the reign of the Messiah to come; he prophesied that "in His name the nations will hope." (Matthew 12:21) Nations pursue humanistic ideologies that are rooted in godless propositions. But the good news is that as cultures crumble and people's lives suffer, the prophecy of Isaiah springs to life, giving an openness to the movement of God's Spirit to people who realize they have been deceived. Iran is a prime example of this.

On the surface, Iranians may not appear to be open to the gospel. The scenes we have seen on the evening news often portray Iranians as religious fanatics who are terrorists. I assure you, however, that behind these images we see in the West are thousands who are disillusioned and broken by the harshness of their lives — people who are seeking God. I was told this story, which illustrates my point. One Iranian pastor stopped in front of a small market to purchase a few items and saw a very stern man standing in front of the store. The man was wearing full Arab-style clothing, showing he was a serious follower of Islam. The pastor thought to himself: *I had better not try to witness to this man; he looks hostile.* Back in his car, his wife suggested he should have given a tract to the hostile man. The pastor, wanting to please his wife, picked up a tract and returned to the hostile man, saying, "Here is the Word of the living God!" The man's face lit up. "Where have you been? God told me to stand here and wait for someone to bring me the word of life. I was just about to give up!" The pastor was shocked but overjoyed that his wife had encouraged him to share the gospel. I love this story because it illustrates the fact that despite outward appearances and beliefs, Iranians are some of the most open people on earth! The fruit of that is in the great awakening taking place in Iran.

The question that must be asked: *What is it that is making Iranians so thirsty for God?*

1. I am convinced that one very large component of this spiritual awakening in Iran has been **prayer**. There have been great prayer movements for Iran for decades. To this day, I meet Americans who, after hearing me talk about what God is doing in Iran, approach me with tears in their eyes to inform me they had been praying for Iran for years. And when I ask them, "Why Iran?" they simply answer, "God just put it on my heart." Also, the missionaries who had labored in Iran for decades had regular prayer times for Iran. One of those missionaries was Dr. William M. Miller. I learned from one of his writings that when he first came to Tehran in the early 1900s, he had the habit of hiking in the foothills of the mountain range, which majestically rises above Tehran to the north. Dr. Miller wrote in his diary that the spiritual condition of the people of Tehran broke his heart, driving him to spend an occasional day in fasting and prayer for a people surrounded not only by the wall of mountains, but by a wall of opposition to the gospel.

2. God has always used the **Christian missionaries** laboring in Iran, from both America and England, for over two hundred years. From the early days, Presbyterian missionaries ministered among the Assyrians in Iran and translated the Bible into modern Assyrian and founded schools to teach the children reading and writing. The reasoning then was that the Assyrians who knew the local languages and the culture would then reach the other people groups of Iran. The sacrifices those early missionaries made are to this day etched in the headstones of a little cemetery in Seer, Iran — a small village near Orumiyeh — as many of the missionaries' children died of diseases due to lack of medical care. As a young boy, my father took me to visit the cemetery where I was deeply moved by the visible representation of the sacrifices those early missionaries had made for the gospel.

The modern missionary movement to Iran focused on two glaring needs. First, the illiteracy rate in those days was estimated to be 85%. If the gospel was going to spread, people had to learn to read, so many schools were started. Second, the low life expectancy was also a major factor because of the many diseases that took the lives of Iranians. The missionaries established many hospitals as an answer to this tragedy. My father and Patty's father served as directors of Christian hospitals in Tabriz, Hamadan, Mashhad, and Rasht. I continue to meet older Iranians who either attended missionary schools or had been born in our hospitals. One Iranian physician confided in me that my father-in-law, Dr. Murray, was like an angel sent by God to heal the sick. Some even said his face was that of an angel because he radiated so much love.

3. Suffering has also played a part in this great awakening, for Iranians have endured great tragedies since the beginning of the Revolution. Many died in the streets during the uprisings against the Pahlavi dynasty. Yet even more died as Khomeini's government purged Iran of any remnants of the Shah's government. Then came the war with Iraq, in which hundreds more died and were heralded as martyrs for the cause of Islam. Today, the prisons in Iran are bursting with political prisoners of whom many are Christians. Suffering breaks people down. It raises questions about beliefs that have been held for generations, leaving them open to new ideas. Many have become atheists and turned to secular hedonism. Others cling to a form of Islam of their own making and follow a god they have created for themselves. But many others are searching for the truth and are ready to hear about Jesus.

4. It is also fair to say that the Islamic regime that has governed Iran for these past years has opened the eyes of many Iranians regarding **the true nature of Islam**. Islam has been deeply ingrained in the hearts and minds of the Iranian people and many believed at the advent of the Islamic Revolution that a new age of prosperity was being issued in. When I was a teenager living in Iran, a University student told me that if Iran ever became Islamic, it would become heaven on earth. After forty years of life under Islamic rule, there is little that resembles heaven. In fact, what would best describe what has occurred is that Islam has been unmasked. Life in Iran is hard in every way. The economic crisis has destroyed the middle class and forced thousands to take drastic measures simply to feed their families.

Desperation has even led to selling one's organs, while others have gone into prostitution, and many more into drug trafficking. Jesus taught it is by our fruit that others will know us and today the Iranian people around the world are witnessing the fruit the Islamic regime has produced.

    5. The good news is that God has not forgotten His promise to the Iranian people. God promised Abraham (Genesis 12) that every nation which blesses the Jewish people would be blessed. In Nehemiah chapter two, we read about how it was an ancient Persian king, Artaxerxes, who bankrolled the restoration of the walls of Jerusalem. There are those who believe that God has been keeping His promise to bless the Persian people for their role in restoring the city of Jerusalem. God has been mightily at work in Iran in these post-Revolution years.

God has been revealing Himself to multitudes of Iranians around the world. The most common experience Iranians testify about is seeing Jesus in a dream. Sometimes they recognize it is Jesus, while at other times they describe a man in a shining white robe. Often, they hear Jesus' invitation to follow Him. He sometimes speaks to them with verses from the Gospels. I am often asked to interpret a dream. Normally, I resist doing that, but many years ago, a Kurdish lady called me and asked if I would interpret her dream. I said I would try. In her dream, she saw herself walking up the steps of what looked like a Greek temple, which was aglow. A strange new joy came over her as she contemplated entering the temple. As she approached the door, a man in white stopped her and informed her she could not enter, for she was unworthy. Her countenance fell. Then the man in white held out a book to her with a large cross inscribed on it. He said, "If you read this book, you will learn how to enter in." At that moment, the interpretation was obvious, so I told her that God loved her and was inviting her to get to know Him, but she would have to read the Bible.

    Along with dreams, Jesus seems to appear in visions. Some have seen outstretched nail-pierced hands as Jesus speaks to them. Another person tried to commit suicide by throwing themselves out of a second-story window; he was pulled back inside by unseen hands. Another person was pronounced dead and remembers the nurse pulling a sheet over his face. At that moment, he heard a voice, "It is not your time," and life returned! When he opened his eyes, he saw the hospital room filled with crosses. Those who have such visions and dreams often become faithful followers of Christ.

Another amazing phenomenon is how God uses His Word, often revealing a verse to someone multiple times. One of the most unique testimonies I have heard was from a lady who said that while she was saying her Muslim Prayers (Namaz), she saw a hand write on the wall these words: "I am the way, the truth and the life." She had never heard these words before, so she called a girlfriend who was a Christian and asked her what she thought they meant. The friend did not have an answer for her, but she invited her to go to church the next Sunday and consult her pastor. As the girl was sitting in the worship service, the pastor began reading from the Bible, "I am the way, the truth and the life." She burst into tears and later gave her life to Christ. Muslims do not believe that one can have a personal relationship with God, but through this experience, this lady discovered to what lengths God would go to personally communicate with her. She now knew God was personal and she could actually know Him through Christ.

Besides dreams, visions, and His Word, God has used miraculous healings to show them His love and mercy. Just as physical healing was a very real part of Jesus' earthly ministry and one sign that the Kingdom of God was at hand, so today Jesus is graciously healing those who are sick and depressed, which frequently leads to their conversion to Christ.

6. Obviously, **modern technology** has also played a strategic role in the great awakening. Satellite television was the first great breakthrough, bringing the gospel to millions of Iranians who could now view Christian programming in the privacy of their own homes. It was nearly impossible for the government to censor this new medium. It became a lifeline for the underground church, which was prohibited from meeting in person with one another. I will never forget the time I was standing in line at Heathrow Airport in London at passport control when a middle-aged woman, wearing a headscarf, turned around and said to me, "Salaam Keshish Tat." (Hi, Pastor Tat!) I was a bit taken aback and asked, "Have we met before?" "Oh no," she replied, "but I know all about you." She told me she had been watching my programs about discipleship on SAT7-PARS and she knew all about me. What she said next made me realize just how important satellite programs were for believers in Iran. She said, "Satellite is all we have!" Not only were the satellite programs sustaining believers, but they were also a wonderful means of sharing the gospel with non-believers. I heard another striking report second hand: one night two women had decided to commit suicide. The doctor had told the mother that she only had a few weeks to live and the daughter could not bear to think of life without her. Sorrowfully, they lit candles and enjoyed one of their favorite meals to prepare for ending their lives. During the meal, they turned on their television to watch what was happening in the world. The first thing they saw was a man speaking passionately. "Whatever you do, do not take your own life!" The mother turned to the daughter and asked, "Who told him?" He went on to share the gospel and invited listeners to call in for prayer. The mother picked up the phone and was soon talking to a counselor who shared more about Jesus. The mother began to pray the sinner's prayer. She turned to her daughter and asked if she, too, wanted to talk to the counselor, but the daughter refused. The next week when the mother revisited her doctor, he gave her the news: "You have been healed!" This news convinced the daughter that Christ was a living Savior and she too committed her life to Christ. These women eventually shared their story with many who were touched by their testimony.

Sometimes as I listen to Iranians giving their testimonies it feels as though I'm a participant in the book of Acts. When Christianity breaks into new cultures and societies, signs and wonders often accompany the preaching of the gospel to prove to its hearers the truth of what they are being told. However, we know that the Christian life is not lived on feelings and on external signs; rather, it depends on a personal relationship with God through Christ and a full dependency on the truth and authority of God's Word.

[I have written a booklet about the secret to ministering to the Iranian community and how to reach their hearts, entitled, "The Keys to the Iranian Heart." (Appendix A)]

NO STRANGER

CHAPTER FIFTEEN
THE CHALLENGES OF THE GREAT AWAKENING

My purpose in writing this book has been to outline my observations over my lifetime regarding the state of Christianity in Iran and among Persian speakers in the Diaspora. I write as an eyewitness reporting what I have seen and understood, not as a historian who might seek to gather a broader picture of what has taken place. In this final chapter I want to present what I believe are some challenges faced by the Persian Church worldwide. Granted, I have not lived in Iran since 1980, but I have:

- lived with Iranians and visited many Iranian pastors and churches

- been called upon to intervene in many church conflicts and struggles

- stood by pastors who have failed morally and needed healing

- been called into churches that have split and tried to understand what types of leadership mistakes led to the crisis

- listened for hours as church members have revealed to me the abuse received at the hands of church leaders

- been a guest speaker in conferences in more countries than I can remember, and

- pastored two Iranian congregations for a total of thirty years.

I have also addressed these issues in seminars, in sermons, and in articles written for Shaban Magazine[16], which was a leadership magazine I founded in 2000 to assist the new generation of Iranian leaders in areas of pastoral theology as well as to outline the skills needed for shepherding the flock of God. I wanted to address issues such as Christian character, one's identity in Christ, and what a wholesome relationship in Christ should be. I longed for new converts to understand how Christ desires to change their marriages and their methods of disciplining their children, along with their methods of leadership.

So, I write as an old soldier who has returned from the battle and desires to assist the new recruits by revealing to them the dangers they will most likely encounter as they press on in ministry. I write as an older brother who loves Christ and His church, who loves Iran and its people and whose heart is filled with gratitude for all the ways the Iranian Church has enriched my life. I long for the current great awakening to bear lasting fruit and bring about a transformation of Iran and its people. This is the background for my next comments.

I have used the term "spiritual tsunami" to describe the great awakening that can take place when God moves. Tsunamis can flood an entire land. Spiritual tidal waves can lift all boats in the harbor at the same time. It is a movement of God in which the Holy Spirit anoints the preaching of His Word causes dead sinners to come alive in Christ. It is a season of deep repentance as God reveals to many their true sinful nature. Amazing signs and wonders often accompany it, as God makes Himself known to unbelievers. It is a time of significant growth for the church as the word spreads about what great things God has done. It brings about reconciliation and healing. New generations of believers with new gifts become leaders as the church matures and new ministries emerge. Can there be any doubt that what is going on in Iran is anything less than a Great Awakening?

In This Holy Seed, the author Robin Daniel documents the challenges the early church faced in North Africa: **what to believe, what to do about persecution, and how to organize as congregations.** In the early church, the crisis of what to believe slowly resolved itself through the many councils and confessions still guiding us. When the intensity of

---

16. www.shabanmag.com

persecution decreased, the church faced the problem of how to relate to those who, under great pressure, had denied Christ but now wanted to return. Finally, the question of order was resolved by the different churches coming under the authority of the Bishop of Rome. Daniel's book is still relevant, as the Persian church today is facing the same three issues.

What to Believe. In college, I took a course on the life and writings of Jonathan Edwards (1703-1758) who lived during and reflected on the Great Awakening that swept through New England in America. He warned that, along with the movement of God, the Enemy produced counterfeit experiences to lead believers astray. These counterfeit experiences were often confused with the genuine work of the Holy Spirit, which always works in conjunction with the Word of God. Herein lies a warning for all who are presently serving Christ and His church among Persian speakers. There will be false teachers peddling their own brand of Christianity as they claim special personal revelations from God. There will be promises made on God's behalf, which, when compared with His Word, were never made. All those who love Christ must be diligent to stay faithful to the Word of God. Knowing what to believe and how to discern false teaching are the most critical components of ensuring doctrinal integrity in a congregation. Edwards also warned that all spiritual tsunamis eventually recede. The day is coming when the urgency for the gospel we now sense among many Iranians will fade; that day will reveal the true faithful disciples of Christ. Therefore, the most important task facing all pastors and teachers today is to mentor and disciple others in the Word of God, that they might be deeply rooted in a personal relationship with Christ and fully grounded in God's Word.

In the pre- Revolution days in Iran, it was much easier to identify the doctrines of the various denominations. Yes, there were differences between the churches; I was a participant in some of the lively discussions that went on regarding those differences. And yes, from time to time there were those who claimed to have a "new word" from the Lord, which contradicted the established churches and the Word of God. Overall, however, it was obvious what each Christian believed. That has changed! Now we define our beliefs by those who we follow; for some it is a particular Satellite TV teacher or a certain preacher. It is similar to the experiences of the Corinthian church. Paul rebuked the church when some claimed they were followers of Apollo, others identified as followers of Peter, and to Paul's dismay, some said they were *his* followers. (I

Corinthians 1:10-17) He points them back to the cross and reminds them they were to be followers of *Christ*. Another significant cause for confusion in the Persian church is how some Iranian leaders have come under the influence of the liberalism so rampant in the West. Sadly, the very churches which in past decades took the Gospel to Iran now reject the authority of the Word of God. Unfortunately, Iranian pastors, wanting to be in step with the Western church, latch on to unbiblical teachings and sow seeds of doubt in the minds and hearts of believers. This notion has led to some becoming universalists, believing that salvation is available to all, regardless of religion, thus denying Jesus' teaching that He is the only way to know the Father. Along with this challenge is the overwhelming influence of the secular, hedonistic culture that has gripped most of western culture. Those schooled in this ideology reject the idea of absolute truth and believe that everyone should be able to do what is right in their own eyes. A young believer explained to me why it was alright for him to live with his girlfriend since that is what all western young people were doing. Last but not least, the emerging Persian church is struggling with syncretism, as new believers bring their Islamic worldview with them when they are converted to Christ. There are multiple ways in which a new believer brings his Islamic beliefs with him, but the one that I believe creates the most damage is his difficulty in comprehending *grace*. There are several Biblical concepts that are hard for a new believer to grasp, such as forgiveness, yet grace seems to me to be the most difficult. One year, I spent several months teaching about grace in the Iranian church. Most could explain to me what the doctrine of grace was, but many still could not let go of the notion that God's love depended on good behavior. It finally occurred to me I needed to share many more real-life illustrations of grace from my own life experiences.

    What is the remedy for dealing with the sea of confusion in which we are adrift? We need godly leaders who are humble servants and who are committed to teaching their flocks to trust the Word of God. As they are faithful to the Scriptures, God will bless their ministries. However, if they do not know the Bible well and depend on their own feelings and interpretations, they will lead people into false teachings and moral confusion. The lessons of the early church should teach us the importance of being a confessional church. A church that depends not only on the teachings of its pastor but is grounded in one of the historic confessions of our faith can weather many more challenges and transitions. We have two wonderful confessions which have been translated into Farsi: The

Heidelberg Confession, and The Westminster Confession of Faith[17] (which was translated by Rev. Tateos Mikaelian who was martyred in Iran for the sake of Christ), which are two very excellent summaries of Biblical truth. I highly recommend both of them.

What to Do About Persecution. The matter of persecution is certainly a very relevant matter for those living in Iran. The emotional and physical trauma that our brothers and sisters are enduring in the prisons of Iran is unimaginable. When I hear how God is sustaining them and using them to minister to others in these dire situations, I am reminded that God always advances the Gospel through trouble. Paul testifies to this through his own imprisonment for the Gospel in Philippians 1:12-18. Let us be diligent in praying for the church in Iran and particularly for those being persecuted for righteousness' sake.

How to Organize in Congregations. What kinds of administrative structures are best suited for the local church and the church at large? This issue has been a challenge with which the church has struggled throughout the centuries. There are three most commonly recognized church structures. One is the *congregational* church in which the seat of authority is found in the congregation itself. Major decisions are decided by the congregation as a whole. It is in some ways the most democratic system. Next is the *Bishop* form of church government, which is a hierarchical form of church government, in which one person is ordained as Bishop and possesses ecclesiastical power to ordain others and appoint pastors to specific churches. This format has dominated a large sector of the modern church and most likely was patterned after the model of Rome's having been the center of political power. Finally, there is the *Presbyterian* form of government in which the congregation elects elders to be empowered to lead the church in spiritual and practical matters. This form of church structure is often called a representative form of government. In the past, we have had all three forms of church government in Iran. I find many believers and even pastors today are not familiar with these time-tested forms of church government, thus falling in step with a form of leadership which grants all authority to a pastor. Given

---

17. The Westminster Confession of Faith was originally translated into Farsi by Rev. Tateos Mikaelian, who was martyred in Iran for the sake of Christ, and reprinted in 2015 (with proof verses and a new layout) by the Jude Project. The Heidelberg Confession was translated by the Jude Project in 2016.

the prominence of this pattern of church governance, it becomes even more crucial to examine what types of leaders we are raising up in the Persian church. I have wrestled with this question my entire ministry. In some ways, it is the most important issue today facing the Persian church because it will determine its future.

Keep in mind that in many ways we are dealing with a first-generation church. Unlike the days in Iran when new believers were folded into a church with history, with a statement of faith and church polity[18]; today's church is more like an amoeba, taking the form of whatever container in which it is placed. Those coming to Christ in Iran are often isolated from physical fellowship with other believers out of fear of persecution. They rely on online teaching and fellowship. There is a great absence of mentors who can disciple new believers. In fact, many fellowships are led by men and women who have been believers for a short time only and have had little or no training. Thus, there are many challenges to church leadership.

Leaders learn to lead from those who led them. Without godly examples to do otherwise, leaders follow the pattern of leadership that is prevalent in Iranian cultures. Leadership in Iran usually means control. When I was planting an Iranian church, I asked one of the elders to make an announcement to the congregation. He resisted. He informed me that there should only be one voice in the church and that should be mine. I believe that the challenges facing the leadership of the Iranian church are: First, they must learn to lead as Jesus did by becoming servant leaders. Servant leaders are humble and teachable, owning their mistakes and demonstrating peacemaking. They recognize that the church's tendency is to elevate them and place them on a pedestal, so they do not teach triumphalism, the teaching that the pastor must never admit to weakness but always give the impression that he is victorious. Second, pastors must be willing to be continually training others for ministry and sharing their ministry with them. God gives spiritual gifts to all believers, and no pastor has them all, even if he believes he does. There is a reason that most Iranian fellowships do not grow beyond 25-40 people; the church is too often a one-man show. Third, many pastors are not accountable to anyone unless they belong to a network or a denomination. Leaders are often led astray in their teaching because they have never learned the principles of

---

18. Or government.

correct Biblical interpretation and have no way of knowing they are going astray and bringing along a congregation with them. Some may tell their church that God is leading them as they drift away from clear Biblical teaching. I was shocked to hear from one pastor who told me that God had revealed to him that God hates Arabs and that he was teaching his church to do the same. Fourth, there is a great need for pastors not to neglect their own families. Their first pastoral responsibility is to their wives. I always try to listen to the concerns of the wives of Iranian pastors. I most often hear: "My husband will drop everything to help a church member but is seldom willing to help me." Or "he prays with the women of the church but he never prays with me." Too often the children are neglected also, so as soon as they are able, they leave the church. This is a larger problem in the Diaspora, in which the parents are functioning as if they are still living in Iran, whereas their children have adopted their host country's culture.

As we wrestle with the challenges facing the modern Persian church, we must never forget that it is Christ's church and the gates of hell cannot prevail against it. We must remember that for many centuries, Christians labored in prayer and faithful witness in Iran hoping to see a day such as we are witnessing today. Knowing this, let us rejoice and worship our sovereign God who is at work and let us do all we can to remain faithful to the Gospel first delivered to the Apostles, of which we have been blessed enough to be recipients. I have been no stranger to what God has been doing in Iran and count that as one of the most wonderful blessings in my life. I have written this chapter, not discouraged by the challenges, but rather I am most hopeful regarding the worldwide Persian church because at its core it is a church in love with Jesus Christ and yearning to share its life with all Persian speakers and I am eager to see how God will move in the years to come.

NO STRANGER

CHAPTER SIXTEEN
PRESSING ON FOR HIS GLORY

Many memories have faded since those boyhood days of growing up in Iran. But the passage of time has not extinguished the passion that burns in my heart for sharing the Gospel with Iranians. Aging may have brought limitations, but it also has brought with it new opportunities. Age brings ministry experience along with the trust of those whom one has served through the years. Having dedicated my life to Christ in my youth and subsequently receiving a call from God to be a minister of the Gospel, I see clearly, now more than ever before, the value of a life committed to Christ and remaining faithful to that calling.

The passage of time reveals a person's identity and motivations. I once performed a funeral service for a man who had no surviving family. Arriving at the funeral home, I was informed that no one would be attending the funeral because the man had had no relatives or friends left. Thus, I preached that day to the funeral director and a room full of empty chairs. James writes, "Blessed is the man who remains steadfast under trial, for when he has stood the test he will receive the *crown of life* which God has promised to those who love him." (James 1:12) James is undoubtedly referring to the Sermon on the Mount and the blessings of life in the Kingdom of God; he is admonishing us to remain faithful during the trials of life in order to receive the promised blessings of a life lived for Christ. In my experience, the blessings have been so plentiful that there would not be space in this short book to mention them all. However, I feel compelled to highlight one blessing that has greatly touched my life: the honor and respect that the Iranian church has given me. God has opened many doors for me to minister to Iranians around the world, and I am continually humbled by Iranian Christian leaders who invite me to teach on their networks in Iran via Zoom. I rejoice when I receive messages from Iranians living in Iran telling me how my writings and sermons have blessed them. For this, I want to give all the glory to God. I say this with some reluctance for fear that some will interpret it as prideful self-promotion, but my intention is that others will be encouraged to press on during difficult times of ministry, trusting that God will use them, too, for His glory. I often speak with discouraged Iranian leaders who feel sidelined and discarded. I pray they will take James' words to heart to "remain steadfast under trial." (James 1:12) Press on with Christ and with His church and remain faithful to Him! Do not let others lead you away from the life-giving teachings of the Bible! Do not give up on people merely because they have disrespected you or turned away from the truth! Keep living for Christ! Watch and wait and you will see the goodness of God in the land of the living.

The Iranian Christian Church in Colorado

Tat and Patty in Colorado

These last few years of my ministry have been in Aurora, Colorado. We moved to Aurora in 1999 in order to be near Patty's parents. We are so glad that we did because we had a wonderful season of life together with them. Patty's parents, who were missionaries in Iran, did not abandon their call to serve Iranians once they returned to America. Sadly, many former missionaries to Iran seemed to lose their interest in the people that God had called them to serve. Not Dr. and Mrs. Thomas Murray! When the Iranian Revolution brought more Iranians to Denver, they hosted a monthly potluck gathering in their home to share love and fellowship with as many Iranian friends as they had. Mrs. Nancy Murray was a gracious hostess and made everyone feel at home as she taught them some hymns of the Iranian church and shared the good news of Christ. Later, they invited Pastor Sobhani, who lived in New York City, to visit their group and help teach this little flock of Iranian seekers. In time, this group grew into what would become the Iranian Christian Church of Colorado, which for the past twenty-five years has met at Faith Presbyterian Church in Aurora, Colorado.

In the late 1990s, the Iranian church called the Rev. Edmond Sarkissian to become their pastor. At this point, a coalition of American Churches banded together to provide the financial expenses of the ministry. Rev. Sarkissian served the Lord faithfully, but as time went on, there was not enough financial support to sustain his family. Thus, when an invitation came from an evangelical Assyrian church in Turlock, California, he felt God's call to move on. His leaving was a sad day for the Iranian Church, but everyone recognized it was God's will. By this time, Patty and I were living in Colorado and had been actively supporting the Iranian Church. Soon after the departure of the Sarkissian family, we met as a church to decide our options for the future. I moderated the meeting and presented three options: one, we could disband and let everyone find American churches to attend. Two, we could downsize to a weekly Bible study. And three, we could continue to have Sunday services. Two very vocal members of the church, brother Heshmat and brother Pasha, were strongly opposed to options one and two. They wanted to continue the Sunday services. They then asked if I would serve as a temporary pastor. I agreed and my "temporary" pastoral assignment has lasted over twenty years! During these years, the church has vacillated between having only a handful of attendees and having every seat filled. I am most grateful for the faithfulness of Brother Heshmat, who has served by my side all these years; in 2022, I was able to take part in his ordination ceremony. He has been a wonderful servant of the Lord and a dear friend. God has been faithful to the Iranian Church. We have seen many come to Christ and many more have heard the Gospel.

During these later years of ministry, God began to bring young Iranian men from other parts of the world into my life. The advent of the Internet made it possible, through platforms like Skype, for me to meet with these young men and mentor them. These mentoring sessions consisted of their sharing their life struggles and theological questions with me, followed by a Bible study together. I had them lead the Bible studies so I could better understand their comprehension of Biblical truths, providing me with insight about which topics and issues we could then address together. We then concluded our time with prayer for each other. It has been a great blessing for me to watch how God has used these men in ministry.

Part of my philosophy was to encourage these men to be folded into a relationship with a good Biblically sound church in their host countries. Many Iranian pastors wanted to remain independent from any host country churches; perhaps out of an apprehensiveness about coming under the control of a western church or perhaps because of linguistic barriers. Whatever the reasoning, it has left many Iranian pastors in the West isolated, which most times resulted in their facing pastoral crises alone. Having no one to turn to for support, these pastors often made poor pastoral choices when problems arose. Without having a church body or church council to come to the aid of a congregation, the inevitable happens, as conflicts and accusations lead to the disintegration of the ministry. Years ago, I made a study of the most commonly found models used by western churches in hosting immigrant fellowships. It is beyond the scope of these pages to discuss all these models, but the model which proved to be the most beneficial for Iranian pastors and churches in western countries was for the host church to accept the Iranian pastor as part of its staff. This relationship provided the benefit of more experienced leaders mentoring the younger Iranian pastor and providing accountability and financial security. The Iranian pastor became part of a leadership team, allowing him to share in regular fellowship and continued education. Whenever I have been able to transfer the man I have been mentoring to an established host church, I am comforted by the fact that I haven't abandoned my disciple but rather, have prepared him to move on to a greater opportunity for success.

Besides mentoring men for the ministry, I have had the challenge of advising Iranian churches in crisis. First-generation Muslim convert churches face countless minefields, especially that of leadership. The concept of "servant leadership" is alien to the Persian cultural understanding of leadership. Some might say that a culture's view of leadership is derived from its view of God. My viewpoint is that Islamic cultures tend to produce "dictators" rather than "servant" leaders. Having noticed the struggles so many first-generation churches have had with their leaders, there is a great need for Biblical teaching of what constitutes servant leadership after the model of our Lord Jesus Christ. This has led me through the years to develop extensive teaching materials on this topic, and I have had the privilege to share it with individual Iranian leaders and in many leadership conferences.

More specifically, I have been called to help train elders and the next generation of leaders for several Iranian churches. I first did this in the Iranian Christian Church of Washington. I have since developed a course for training elders. Sometimes, I have been invited to attend elder meetings of specific churches in order to aid in conflict resolution when conflict has arisen over theological differences and leadership challenges. Frequently, I have been called to assist a church when the pastor has committed adultery. It is devastating for a church when their pastor is caught in the sin of adultery and a very challenging ministry situation to walk into. I have spent hours listening to the pain of church members and ministering God's grace to them. On other occasions, I have been called in when a church split has occurred and was asked to comfort the remnant. All these experiences drove me to realize how weak I was and how much I needed Christ's wisdom and grace. But it also showed me that Christ's church is always under attack; God used these troubled times to advance His kingdom in me and in the churches I sought to serve.

Discipleship Training

My calling has always been in discipling new believers and encouraging spiritual formation in the Iranian church. This passion led me to write eleven booklets on various practical topics that are available in Farsi online (Shabanmag.com). I taught a course for PARS Theological Centre on the principles of making disciples for Christ and a Farsi version of "Cubs to Lions," a discipleship course for Muslim-background believers written by George Houssney of Horizons International. As with most ministries, I have been using more social media to make disciples. I use Instagram to interact with Iranian believers in various parts of the world and to share in viewer follow-up for the Christian satellite: SAT-7 PARS.

During this season of ministry, Patty has also continued her passion for leading the Iranian church in worship. Patty has a genuine gift for ministering through song. She expanded her ministry of music by recording herself, singing traditional Persian hymns and putting them on

YouTube. We have had wonderful feedback from those who have been blessed by her music.

Equipping The American Church

God has opened many doors for me in equipping the American church to be more effective in reaching Muslims. I have taught "Perspective Classes" for over thirty years in many cities in the US and Canada. On one occasion, the Canadian Bible Society asked me to share with their national staff how to build bridges of love with Muslims. Locally, I have taught in partnership with Horizons International a course entitled "Engaging Islam." This has led to many opportunities of meeting with missionary candidates to the Muslim world and helping to prepare them for a more effective ministry. I have particularly enjoyed the times when I am asked by American missionaries to present the Gospel in Persian to an Iranian seeker. I was once asked to contact an Iranian College student who was asking many questions about Christianity. When I called the student, I began by speaking English, but when I sensed he was struggling to express himself, I switched to Farsi. He began to cry; he was so relieved that I spoke his language that we spent the next hour on the phone as I shared the Good News and answered his questions. Since I also speak Azeri, one of our missionary families had an Azerbaijani family staying with them in Europe and they were having a hard time communicating with each other, so they contacted me. I had the joy of being able to share the Gospel with this family. On another occasion, I received a phone call from an Iranian in an immigration prison who wanted to know about Jesus. He could only talk for ten minutes at a time, so he would call me repeatedly. I discipled him for several weeks and then one day he showed up in the Iranian church in Colorado. This is just a small sampling of the ways God has used me to be a bridge of love into the lives of people from Iran, Afghanistan, and Azerbaijan.

It is fitting, as I come to the end of my book, for me to give thanks to its actual author. My story is a small part of the larger redemptive plan that God has had for the people of Iran. It was the Lord who called my parents to Iran in 1947, for it was God's purpose that I grow up in a country that was not my own in order that I might one day be able to relate the Good News to them. It was God who brought Patty and me back together after growing up in Iran and provided me with a wife who also knew the language and culture of Iran. It was God's perfect timing when we returned to Iran in 1979 to become eyewitnesses to the changes that Islamic Revolution was imposing on the people of Iran and also to observe the first tremors of the spiritual awakening that was in the making. It was God who brought us back to America in 1980, to take what we had learned from the Persian church in Iran and serve Iranians in the Washington, D.C. area. It was God who called me to leave a wonderful American pastorate to become the pastor of eighteen first-generation Iranian Christians who were from a Muslim background. It has been the blessing of God that has led many faithful Christians throughout our years of ministry to support Patty and me, both financially and with their prayers. Finally, it has been God who honored His Word and bathed it with His Holy Spirit that has resulted in the fruit that we have seen. Therefore, Patty and I give God all the glory for the great things He has done.

NO STRANGER

APPENDIX:
THE KEYS TO THE IRANIAN HEART
BY TAT STEWART

"Yet I will restore the fortunes of Elam in the days to come, declares the Lord."
Jeremiah 49:39

When the history of Iran in the twentieth century is written, the year 1979 will be seen as a defining watershed. The events that unfolded that year have forever changed the lives of the Iranian people. That was the year that the Shah of Iran, Reza Pahlavi was forced to abdicate his long reign in Iran and flee into uncertain exile. It was also the year that Ayatollah Rouhollah Khomeini flew into Iran on his chartered Air France jumbo jet and established the Islamic Republic of Iran. These events shocked the Iranian people as no other event in modern times has.

As when an earthquake sends out shock waves, the events of 1979 sent out its own series of shock waves. The people of Iran at best could have been called nominal Muslims but now the full weight of Islamic Law and practice was laid on them. Women were forced once again to cover themselves with the "chador", a veil that covers from head to toe. All alcoholic beverages were destroyed, movie theaters were closed, and western music was eliminated from the radio and T.V. programming. A countrywide reform was begun to bring every area of personal and public life into compliance with Islamic Law. It is far beyond the scope of this brief article to try to give a full description of the revolutionary changes that came to Iran, suffice it to say that the Islamic Revolution turned life upside down in Iran.

The results were catastrophic. Iranian society began to erupt. Thousands of educated Iranians and those with ties to the previous regime began to flee the country.

It was difficult to book a seat on a flight out of Iran. The great Iranian Diaspora was on. It is interesting to note that in Jeremiah 49:34-39 we read that God will bring His judgment against the Elamites (one of the ancient names for the Iranians) and He will humiliate their king and scatter them to the ends of the earth. In the 17 years since the Islamic Revolution, Iranian people have literally been scattered to every continent of the globe. A 1993 study done by the Iranian Christian Internationals, Inc., shows significant numbers of Iranians in 33 different countries and on every continent. The total number of Iranians scattered worldwide is cited at over 3 million. Today that number has climbed to 4 million. It is estimated that 2 million of these displaced Iranians live in North America.

The next shock wave that began to be felt was the surge of Iranians who began to turn to Christ as a result of the Revolution. Of course, this was not evident to all at first as many Christians fled Iran along with others. My wife and I had the privilege to be in Iran that first year of the Revolution and we were firsthand witnesses to the devastation that the exodus of Iranian Christians had on the churches; however, at the same time we saw the heightened interest in the Christian faith as churches began to be filled up with seekers. Iranian Christians International reports the number of Iranian believers in 1979 at just fewer than 3,000.

Today, 17 years later, estimates range from 25,000 to 40,000. It is really very difficult to get statistics which can be verified but the point is clear: there has been a dramatic growth of Christianity among Iranian Muslims. In 1969 Dr. William M. Miller wrote his landmark book entitled, <u>Ten Muslims Meet Christ</u>, and it was heralded as a breakthrough. Today if Dr. Miller were to write a book he would have to call it the rise of the Muslim convert church; for since the Islamic Revolution over fifty Iranian fellowships have arisen outside of Iran; this fact prompting Greg Livingstone, the founder of Frontiers Missions, to comment that the Iranian Church is the most mature Muslim convert church in the world. Iranians are coming to Christ in unprecedented numbers with more of them turning to Christ in the last 17 years than in the previous 1,000 years.

The Iranian harvest field is white and awaiting workers. Today there is only one Christian worker for every one million Iranian.

There was one more shock wave yet to consider in understanding the Iranian context and that was the persecution of the church in Iran. The Christians in Iran fled from the grip of the Islamic Revolution because they intuitively knew Islam's stance on Christianity. They knew firsthand that Islam would make every effort to stamp it out. Again, it is beyond the scope of this article to go into depth in describing the persecutions that the Iranian church has undergone; suffice it to say that five pastors have been martyred since the beginning of the Revolution and countless others have been persecuted and martyred. Today Iranian believers are routinely persecuted for their faith. The blood of the martyrs has indeed become the seeds of revival. Pastor Mehdi Dibaj, one of those martyred for Christ, often said, " The Church in Iran is like a rose petal; the more you press it the sweeter the perfume."

In summary, the Islamic Revolution has changed the contour of the Iranian's mind and heart. He has been driven from his homeland by forces beyond his power to control or even to understand. He has been ripped from the close and intimate relationships of his family, causing devastating emotional consequences. He has suffered the ravages of war and possibly has had members of his family executed by the Islamic courts. He has witnessed the unmasking of Islam and may now hate all religion and religious leaders. He may mistrust other Iranians and want to lose himself in his new country of residence. He is a stranger living in a new culture. If he does not know the language he must work for other Iranians and be at their mercy for survival. Many Iranians living in the west are well educated but have had to settle for very menial occupations while still others have become very successful in a great variety of careers and make great contributions to our society as productive citizens, but the events of the Islamic Revolution still affect them deeply and stir up a host of basic questions about the God of history and the purpose of life. You will find within the Iranian community the full range of conclusions about life but you will also find some of the most open and searching souls on earth. God has prepared them for such an hour and He is calling us in the Western church to respond.

You will not regret the time you give to your Iranian friend for he will teach you much more about friendship than you will be able to teach him. You will find him more interested in spiritual matters than your western neighbor probably is and you will find that God may well touch your life afresh through him as you observe God at work in him.

The Key of God's Love

By now it should not come as a surprise when I tell you that your Iranian friend needs love. You can see that he has been greatly hurt. He has lost so much; he has lost his homeland and probably his life's fortunes. By the time he gets to the west he may well have been abused by smugglers who promised him an easy access to the west and he has experienced many harassments by western government officials. He needs a friend who can love him with the unconditional love of Christ. He needs someone who can help him find his way in his new country.

As I listen to the countless testimonies of Iranian Christians, one of the keys that God has used in their lives was the unconditional love of Christians. Iranians are very social people and do not thrive on being alone. They would rather be with a group of people than alone. When they come to the west they are amazed at how separatist we are. They may find us to be friendly on the surface but are surprised at how poor we are at friendships. When they come to our churches we smile and greet them but we seldom invite them to our homes or open our lives to them. This would not be the case if we were in their home country; we would very quickly be invited to their homes. When we understand this about their culture it becomes a key bridge into the Iranian's heart. Become his friend! Open your life to him. Learn about his culture and enjoy his foods. One aspect of Iranian culture that you must quickly master if you are going to have successful interaction is what Iranians call "tarof". The best way I can explain "tarof" is to say that it is a formal politeness that may disguise the true feelings of the person. For example, if you ask your Iranian friend if he would like something to eat, he will probably say no. However, what you should do is bring him something to eat anyhow. He is not likely to share with you his real wants. If you go to his house it is customary to take flowers or a small gift. The best thing to do is to ask you Iranian friend to tell you about how "tarof" works. For a fuller description of the Iranian culture and holidays, I would recommend <u>Sharing the Gospel with Iranians</u>, by Don M. McCurry.

The Key of God's Truth

The events of the Islamic Revolution have caused a great many Iranians to be disillusioned with religion. They have seen the hypocrisy of their religious leaders. They know the powerlessness of Islam to change the human heart. As I have listened to dozens of testimonies I hear this theme over and over again. Their disillusionment is with the "Mullahs" who rule Iran with merciless adherence to the Koran. Many of them have a story to tell you about their discovery of the emptiness of Islam. They might tell you about their experiences of searching for the truth and how they brought their questions to the Mullah, who told them to believe blindly.

One on my good friends who taught the Koran for many years, who today is a follower of Jesus Christ, shared with me how he had been taught that if he would repeat a certain verse from the Koran a thousand times God would give him anything he desired. He prayed and fasted for three days and repeated the verse thousands of times.

He told God there was only one thing that he desired and that was for God to change his character. He had a terrible temper. Once he had finished his spiritual exercise he had great hope that God would answer and make a new man out of him. When he emerged from his room he saw one of his children doing something annoying and he exploded with anger. Within moments he was in great despair for, not only had he gotten anger but he had discovered his faith was powerless to change him. So great was his despair that he plotted to take his life. Instead he was led to the cross of Christ and to the One who makes all things new. Iranians are experiencing a great paradigm shift in their souls. They are going through a time of great questioning and the key to witnessing to them is to present the truth in love.

It is extremely important to note at this point that all our confessions of the truth must be accompanied with a life that demonstrates it as well. They have been so disillusioned by religion and religious leaders that they will not easily be convinced by insincere Christianity. It is the reality of Christ, which they are seeking, not a formal nominal Christianity. This must put us on the alert to be the fragrance of Christ. You can begin to demonstrate Christ's reality in your life by praying with your Iranian friend. I usually say something like this. "I like to pray with my friends; would it be alright if we close our time together with prayer?" Never once has an Iranian objected. When I pray I always make it a very personal and intimate communication with God because I know that they do not know

God that way. I also always include very specific requests for my friend. God is so faithful and almost always answers those prayers. Our prayer times serve as a spiritual lab session in which they see how much I depend on God and they see God at work. It does not surprise me when my Muslim friend calls back to tell me God answered my prayers and would I be willing now to pray for another matter? Now I have an open door to begin to share with him how he can know God as I do. As you can see, I have not argued my friend towards faith in Christ but have led him to "taste and see that the Lord is good." (Psalm 34:8 NIV)

As we pursue this matter of truth the good news is that in general, Iranians still believe in absolute Truth and revelation. (The exception here is if the Iranian has completed his formal education in the west; then he may well have become a western relativist). They have been taught that the "Injil" (The Gospels) is a holy book and that they should read it. They may have been told that it has been tampered with but my experience is that they are anxious to read it. I find that Iranians gladly accept a gift of the New Testament. Sometimes I will say something like, "Now that you are living in our country you probably would like to know what Christians really believe." Then I will present them with a New Testament. I am always careful to caution them from thinking that all westerners are Christians. I go on to tell them that as they read they should underline the sections that are hard for them to understand. I assure them that it is all right to make marks in the Bible since it is a guidebook to God and His peace. This may come as a surprise for them since they revere the Koran but seldom read it let alone write in it. The first verse I like to read to an Iranian seeker is Matthew 11:28-30. The Lord's invitation to give rest to those who are weary and burdened always seems to cut to their hearts.

Two cautions are in order here. One, you must be forewarned that the Iranian's mind is very much a literal mind. By that I mean he will take the Bible very literally and you will have to help him understand it. Be patient as he asks you questions you may never have heard before. An example might be something like this. "You say Jesus is God but here he is praying to God. Now if he is God whom is he praying to?" Iranian seekers also will need help with many terms that are very familiar to us. They will not know what a Pharisee is or what the Jewish feasts are all about. As you encourage your Iranian friend to read and ask questions be very patient and explain everything. Do not assume he is getting the message on his first reading. It is better that you discuss these things with him alone. Never ask him questions about his faith in front of other Iranians but set times to be alone with him. It is also better that he initiates these times. Iranians are very polite and may agree to meet with you just to please you. So tell your Iranian friend that you are at his service for when he wants to discuss his Bible reading. As this point the best thing you can be doing is to be praying for him.

The second caution is that the Iranian tends to see Truth not so much as objective Truth but embodied in a position or person. For example, a young Christian might give a seeker a totally correct answer from the Scriptures but the seeker will not accept it as truth because it did not come from the mouth of the pastor. This means that you should find a way to link the Iranian seeker with a person whom he accepts as authoritative in the matter. Take him to your pastor or an older leader in the fellowship and let him get his answers from him. This is especially important if the Iranian you are dealing with is an older man.

Now we are ready to get down to some specific discussions with our Iranian seeker. At this point I cannot overemphasize how important it is not to debate the weaknesses of Islam. It is far more productive to use the New Testament and simply discuss who Christ is and what He offers the sinner. It is also advisable to present Christ as Savior of sinners and leave the question of His divinity for later.

The first problem you may to run into is that in the mind of your Iranian friend, the terms you are using mean different things. You may not pick this up at first but it is a major hurdle that must be overcome. For example, when you suggest that your friend is a sinner he may well become quite insulted. The reason for his indignation is that in his mind sins are horrible crimes against God like murder, adultery and stealing. He is insulted that you are suggesting that he is such a person. You will need gently to go to Genesis and show him the story of the Fall and explain that he may well be a good person in comparison to other human beings but in God's sight all have sinned and he has inherited his sin from Adam and Eve. You will have to show him that all human beings are sinners not because they sin; but they sin because they are sinners. I often spend an entire evening laying a sure foundation on the depravity of man.

As you continue your discussions with your Iranian friend you will want to begin to define for him, from the scriptures, many key terms. Jesus' true identity will quickly become a focal point. He will say that he believes in Jesus. But before you celebrate his conversion, you need to know what it is that he believes about Jesus. He believes he was a great prophet, that he was born of a virgin and that he lived a sinless life and that Jesus Himself did not die on a cross for us, rather is was someone who looked like him. Jesus ascended into heaven before the so-called crucifixion. Now you realize you are up against a system of thought that has carefully eclipsed Jesus's divinity and atonement. All your arguments will not reveal the truth of Christ to your Muslim friend; it will take the revealing work of the Holy Spirit.

A day will come when your Iranian friend will want to have a serious discussion with you about the Divinity of Christ. He may now find himself drawn to Christ but the Trinity is his stumbling block. Here are the steps I have used that God has blessed many times.

1. "Do you agree that God is Almighty and can do anything He wills?"

2. "Do you agree that God is a Spirit and can take any shape he wills?"

3. "Do you agree that God is infinite and beyond human comprehension except that He chose to reveal Himself to us?"

I have yet to meet an Iranian who disagreed with these statements. After laying the foundation I share this illustration. I ask him to compare the vastness of the ocean with that of God. We cannot possibly explore the entire ocean. But what if I took a glass and filled it with water from the Ocean and brought it to you? Now you can taste it, touch it and smell it. You could put it under a microscope and you would see that in essence it is the same as the ocean. It is separate from the ocean but it is in essence the same as the ocean. Then I read John 1:1, 14 and Colossians 1:15. I show how God emptied Himself and became a human being so that we could taste and see who He is. This illustration has been the key for many Iranians to begin to understand the Divine nature of Christ. Throughout your discussion you will want underscore the Christians belief in one God by reading him I Corinthians 8:6

You will need to carefully help him see what the Scriptures teach about the character of God, the nature of heaven, salvation, grace and faith. You can safely assume that he has non-Biblical concepts for most of these precious truths.

When you talk about prayer, his experience is with the recited memorized prayers in Arabic that he really doesn't understand and that while he is praying his mind is wandering. When you begin to pray with him he might even repeat what you are saying because he has never really talked to God. This is to illustrate how important it is to get your Iranian seeker into the Word. Be sure to provide him with good solid evangelical literature in Persian.

One very good resource is Dr. Miller's little book, <u>The Beliefs and Practices of Christians</u>, in Persian.

The Key of God's Touch

In our arsenal of weapons that we have with which to share Christ with Iranians, we still must look at our greatest weapon. The greatest weapon we have is that God has chosen to touch the Iranian people at this point in history. We know that Jesus told Peter that it was not flesh or blood that had revealed to him that Jesus was the Christ rather it was the Spirit of God. Today the Spirit of God is touching Iranians around the world. That means that God has already gone before you in witnessing to the Iranians in your city.

As you grow close to Iranians you will hear more and more stories about the dreams they may be having. You may find these stories hard to grasp but I have found that almost every Muslim convert that I know has had some type of dream that he understood to be a revelation of Christ. These dreams seem to awaken a hunger for Christ. I have come to see them as God's calling His own out of the world because we, His church, have failed to go to the Muslim world as we were commanded to go. Still today only 2% of the western mission force is serving among the Muslims who make up of 20% of the world's population. The approach I take with these dreams is to celebrate them and then invite them to get to know Jesus through reading the New Testament.

Over the years I have catalogued the types of dreams that Iranians are having about the Lord. Most of them have a rescue motif. The person is drowning and a hand comes down into the water and saves him. A person is ill and a person in radiant white robes enters his room and tells him he will be healed and he is. Not only do they have dreams; they also may have visions while awake. The point is that God is calling these dear people and we need to be sensitive to the work of the Holy Spirit and be ready to follow up with good Biblical discipleship.

The other evidence of the touch of God is the stories of the transformation of those who have been saved. Iranian Christians have miraculous testimonies. I never get tired of hearing them. Their testimonies are full of stories of how God intervened in their lives. One Iranian man told me that while he was visiting Los Angeles, he was walking the streets to pass the time of day when a painter on a ladder said "hello" to him. That began a two-hour conversation that led him to trust Christ. He confessed, "God sought me out."

I encourage you to get to know the Iranian Christians in your city and have them tell you about how they came to faith in Jesus. It will thrill you. The next very important step is to introduce your Iranian Christian friend to your seeker friend. There is no power like the testimony of one Iranian believer telling his story to another. Another important insight is that if you feel you have led an Iranian to Christ and he refuses to meet with other Iranians, it may well be a sign that he has not really come to faith. A good acid test of true faith is that one is willing to confess Christ before his own peers.

If you need help in locating Iranian Christians in your city get in contact with I.C. I. at 719-596-0010 and they will assist you.

There is another powerful testimony to the touch of God in the Iranian community — the Iranian Church itself. Where true Iranian believers gather for worship and fellowship is another tool you want to use in reaching Iranians. The Muslim who attends a worship service in Persian usually makes comments like, "I have never experienced such peace!" In our Persian language fellowship, we have many Muslims who come to church just to feel the peace of the presence of God. But there is yet another unseen difference that you and I as westerners probably will miss and that is the different social flavor a gathering of Iranian believers has in comparison with a secular gathering of Iranians. I have heard numerous times from Iranians, as they tell me their testimonies, that it was the transformed relationships in the Iranian Body of Christ that convinced them that Christ was real.

There is no doubt about it; Iranians have been uniquely prepared for the Gospel. God has brought them to our shores and He is calling us to be available to minister to them. In many of our larger cities there is probably a small fellowship of Muslim convert Iranian Christians already worshipping and fellowshipping. If we are open to God's Spirit we can be God's link between the unbelieving Iranian and the Iranian Church. It might surprise you that an unbelieving Iranian would rather have you as his friend than having one of his own unknown countrymen as a friend. We need to use this favored position that we as westerners hold and use it for the advancement of our Lord's Kingdom.

NO STRANGER

MINISTRY RESOURCES BY TAT STEWART

Discerning the Will of God
This booklet surveys the wrong ways believers often approach discerning what God's will is and gives very practical ways to discover what God's will is and where God gives the believer freedom to make his own choices.

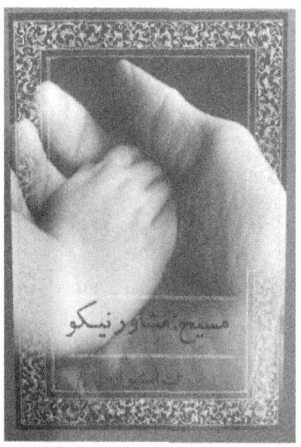

Christ the Good Counselor
This booklet examines the Biblical solution to dealing with troubling emotions like fear, worry, anger, un forgiveness etc and gives step by step ways to receive Christ's counsel.

Raising Children God's Way

Most parents use various methods to modify the unpleasant behavior of their children; such as bribes, threats and emotional manipulation. But the Bible teaches us to train our children in the things of the Lord and lead them to faith in Christ before we can expect them to behave as Christians. Methods of time-tested disciplines are discussed.

The Search for Significance

In this booklet the longing for meaning and significance is addressed. The false ways the world encourages us to find value and purpose compared to the way God does. It challenges the reader to discover the value God gives us and to cling to those things we cannot lose.

Christian Marriage

This booklet begins with how to discern God's will in who you marry and follows up with giving the Biblical reasons for marriage and what are the keys to becoming one flesh. The marks of a marriage in trouble are discussed with suggestions how to maintain intimacy God's way.

Biblical Worship

Worship is our response to the person and work of God through Christ and the Holy Spirit. What are the forms of unacceptable worship in the Bible and what is the characteristic of worship that pleases God? What are the fruit of those who truly worship God in Spirit and Truth?

The Power of Biblical Forgiveness
In this booklet the reader will be confronted with all the reasons we give for not forgiving others and learn just how vital forgiving others is to their own spiritual life. This booklet has been widely used by God to set believers free from the bondage of unforgiveness.

Discerning God's Call to Ministry
The purpose of this booklet is to assist those who are wondering if they are called to be leaders in Christ's church. How God called men and woman in the Bible is examined, as well as the inner call a person might feel and the role the Body of Christ plays in discerning one's call.

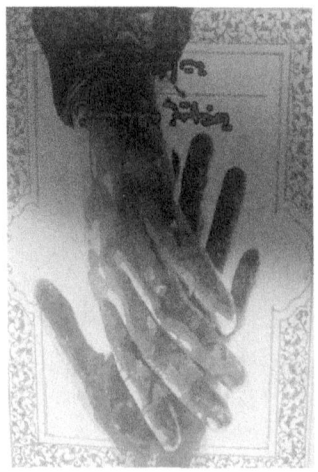

Equipping the Saints

The purpose of this booklet is to help a pastor teach congregations about motivational spiritual gifts so that he can assist them in finding ministries within the body of Christ. (based on Romans 12:3-8)

Preaching Biblically

The purpose of this booklet is to teach young preachers how to preach Biblical truth in ways that connect with the listener, how a preacher needs to prepare his own heart as well as to strive to first understand the text, and how to balance his preaching points with illustrations that reach the heart of his listener.